Arras, 1917

ARRAS, 1917

THE JOURNEY TO RAILWAY TRIANGLE

Walter Reid

BIRLINN

This edition published in
Great Britain in 2011 by
Birlinn Limited
West Newington House
10 Newington Road
Edinburgh EH9 1QS

Copyright © Walter Reid 2003

First published in 2003 by
Tuckwell Press Ltd as
To Arras, 1917: A Volunteer's Odyssey

ISBN 978 1 84341 054 6
e-book ISBN 978 0 85790 055 5

British Library Cataloguing-in-Publication Data
A catalogue record is available
on request from the British Library

Typeset by Antony Gray
Printed and bound in Great Britain by
CPI Antony Rowe, Chippenham, Wiltshire

To The Memory of
ERNEST REID
and for
JANET, JULIA & BRYONY

Contents

Illustrations

Ernest Reid

Ernest's grandparents and their children

Tom Reid, Ernest's father

Sir Hugh McPherson

Hazelwood, the Reid family home

Paisley Grammar School

The Cameronians' war memorial

Aerial reconnaissance photograph of Railway Triangle

The objectives for the first day of the Battle of Arras

Fixing scaling ladders in the trenches

Moving out of an assembly trench

British troops at Feuchy

A wounded Scottish officer

Wounded men at Feuchy

The Duchess of Westminster's Hospital, Le Touquet

Alexander Black

Ernest's grave, Étaples

Monchy-le-Preux

The military cemetery, Étaples

Ernest's gravestone, Étaples

Foreword

This book was conceived as a short memoir of Ernest Reid, who died in 1917, of wounds sustained in the Battle of Arras.

But as I wrote, I found that it was necessary to put his small part in the 1914–18 war into the context of a conflict of which many people only have a series of disjointed images. Much more significantly, the scope of the book extended itself as I realised how foreign the cultural and intellectual institutions of a hundred years ago would be, if not to my children's generation, then certainly to the next. And so, I have endeavoured to put Ernest's life into its moral as well as its historical context, to try to describe the climate in which he grew up, and the influences which formed him and his generation, the generation which supplied the subalterns of the Great War. As a result, although the book remains primarily a biography of its subject, it also explores the spirit in which Britain, still essentially Victorian, went to war in 1914.

To a large extent that spirit had evaporated by 1939, and I do not think it can be said to exist in the conflicts of our time. That is not necessarily a change to be deprecated, but it is worth considering the fact that the officer class, and to an extent the other ranks, in the First World War were imbued with a notion of duty and a code of behaviour that in its way was as remarkable and is now as obsolete as the chivalric rules of medieval combat.

This code, this submission to duty, formed a generation for their rôle and determined their fate in the carnage of the Western Front. And it is for that reason, and not just because we know its end from the beginning, that the story of Ernest Reid and his contemporaries is ineffably sad.

Acknowledgements

It has been a surprise and delight to encounter the readiness of scholars and other experts to give generously of their time and to share their knowledge and experience.

I have to record a great debt of gratitude to the late Lord Jenkins of Hillhead, OM. He read and revised the typescript of the book, and without his support it would not have been published. Even at the end of his life his enthusiasm and his intellectual vigour were enormous. I am very grateful to him.

Sir Martin Gilbert, CBE, and Professor T. C. Smout, CBE, Historiographer Royal in Scotland, read the book in draft form and it has benefited hugely from their revisions. Their suggestions have resulted in the excision of many mistakes (though the responsibility for surviving solecisms is mine). I greatly appreciate their help and encouragement.

I wish to express my gratitude to: Malcolm Balen, Professor Neil Blain, Donald Browarski-Beaucamp, Dr Christopher Dowling and Liz Bowers of the Imperial War Museum, Dr Jennifer Felderhof, Professor Niall Ferguson, J. Melvyn Haggarty, Head of History and Archivist, Paisley Grammar School, the Staff of the Mitchell Library, Glasgow, Major R. J. W. Proctor, M.B.E., late of the Black Watch Regiment, Moira Rankin, Senior Archivist, University of Glasgow, Thomas B. Smyth, Archivist, the Black Watch Regiment, Lieutenant-Colonel Richard Taylor, late of the King's Own Scottish Borderers, Judith Vickers and Frances Walsh.

I am grateful to Doris Nisbet, my secretary for 26 years, for making these 26 years of work much more fun than they would otherwise have been, for turning my incoherent dictation and illegible handwriting into an elegant typescript, and for rescuing the scrapbook that is referred to in the text.

My daughters, Dr Julia Reid and Bryony Reid, respectively proof-read and helped me with the Bibliography; and I am grateful to them for that and for the interest they have taken in this book. It would not be quite true to say that it would not have been written but for them, but they certainly were in my thoughts when the idea first took root in my mind. My final thanks are reserved for my wife, Janet: for her support and for being the gentlest and most perceptive of editors – and for, always, being Janet. It is not inappropriate that I should conclude on this domestic note: as I have written this book I have reflected on how very fortunate I have been to be blessed with a happy family and family life, something which was to be denied to Ernest and so many of his contemporaries. And so, while the first dedication of this work is of course to the memory of Ernest, no less heartfelt is the second: to Janet, Julia and Bryony.

1

The Silent Shore

THE START OF THE SEARCH

Ernest Reid died on 18 April 1917, twenty-seven years before I was born. He was the uncle I never knew. And yet over the years my thoughts have turned more often to him than to the uncles that I did know and love. In some ways I have come to know him better than them, and his life and death and memory have perhaps been consciously or unconsciously a greater influence on me than theirs.

Long before this memoir was in gestation – indeed from my earliest days – Ernest was present in our household, rarely spoken of, and then in tones of poignant respect.

He was the middle of the three brothers of whom my father, Ronald, was the youngest. There were five years between each of the brothers, so that Douglas, ten years older than Ronald, must have been an old older brother, without fitting in to another recognisable category, like that of uncle. Ernest on the other hand, just five years older, was accessible; but older by enough to be contemplated without sibling rivalry. He was an epitome of that golden Edwardian generation, popular, intellectually able and athletic, and Ronald simply idolised him.

Ronald was fifteen when Ernest died, and he never truly got over his death. I do not mean that he remained broken-hearted or incapable of throwing himself wholeheartedly into the fun of life. On the contrary, he lived life with gusto and zest. But he did not ever adjust to Ernest's death in the sense of seeing it as a simple historical event, free from a sense of tragedy and of unfulfilled destiny.

He rarely brought himself to speak of Ernest, and when he did so it was without revealing much that was personal. When he, who had rarely been ill before and was rarely to be ill thereafter, had a heart attack on a family holiday in Arran in 1963, and remained in bed while my mother, Elsie, my sister, Judith, and I ate together in the hotel diningroom, Elsie, perhaps impressed by the singularity of the circumstances and struck by intimations of mortality, recalled that when she and Ronald had married, he had discussed other members of his family, but said to her that he would tell her about Ernest on another occasion. He had never brought himself to do so. That is all the more remarkable because in the long nights in their air raid shelter during the Second World War their recreation was for Elsie, at least, to take one member of her family each night and relate their peculiar history and interesting foibles. But although, for instance, they might explore the (interesting) history of Aunt Lizzie, Ernest was not talked about. (Aunt Lizzie, a very early lady motorist, a talented amateur cabinetmaker, a nurse in the First World War, was a strong character. When her fiancé was reported to be on holiday on the Isle of Man with another woman, she went there at once to see for herself. On her return she simply said, 'I never want to hear his name again'. She unpicked his initials from the table linen that had been assembled for their marriage, and she remained a spinster for life.) It was largely from Dorothy, the first wife of Ronald's cousin Dewar, that Elsie learned what she did of Ernest: how he was admired by his contemporaries, and how he appears to have excelled as much at school and university as on the games field.

There were other glimpses of Ernest. First, and most literally, there were the photographs: quite a number, though all of his time in the Army; no photographs exist of Ernest as a schoolboy or a student. Some were framed and some were not, but none was displayed in our house. They lay in drawers and shelves. We were all aware of them, but they were never mentioned. More than his brothers and unlike the following generation, he has the clean-cut, level-eyed good looks that seem to have been issued to the First

World War subalterns along with their Sam Browne belts and their swagger-sticks. But the impression is not of intolerable *Boy's Own Paper* manliness: there is strength of character and a set jaw, but there is humour and warmth in the eyes and the lips.

The impression his portrait gives is of a strong man, but a man it would have been good to be with, especially in such circumstances as those in which he spent the last years of his life. But this reassuring reaction would be dissipated, and poignancy would break in again, with the next photographs in the pile: images of graves – first the simplest of wooden crosses, then a rather stark headstone, and finally that same headstone surrounded and softened by mown grass and roses: the livery of what became the Commonwealth War Graves Commission.

A second image was of a brown leather suitcase filled with Ernest's letters to his parents: written perhaps weekly, in military lead pencil, initially from training camps in Britain such as Nigg in Ross-shire; and later from France, from the trenches and from Rest Camps. Even without trespassing on the privacy of these communications, which I never did, it was difficult to contemplate this correspondence without being moved by the circumstances in which it was written and the combination of heartache and delight with which it must have been received.

A final glimpse, and in some ways the saddest, was the annual ritual which continued in our house until perhaps the end of the 1950s – that is, for more than forty years after Ernest's death – of placing a poppy wreath on the War Memorial by Sir Robert Lorimer at Paisley Cross, a powerful piece of imagery that re–presents a chivalric mounted knight sculpted by A. Meredith Williams going to war surrounded by an escort of World War One infantrymen in their gas capes and tin helmets.

The wreath was a large one, composed of huge, waxy poppies. It was inscribed (always in 'indelible pencil') to the memory of Acting Captain Thomas Ernest Reid of the Black Watch Regiment, and it would remain along with innumerable others on the plinth of the Memorial until even the indelible pencil became illegible.

These were the images of Ernest that I knew as a child, and this was the atmosphere in which his memory came to me. The memory was not pervasive. It was only one, and far from the most important one, of many influences and atmospheres and cultural pressures that consciously or not I absorbed. But it was there. It was not expressed, and what is important is precisely that it remained unexpressed: that a vacuum of communication existed around someone who was so important to Ronald. What I did feel, not strongly, not worryingly, but I think quite clearly, was that I, and perhaps all of us, were not entirely worthy of Ernest.

Why did I not ask – ever, at all – about Ernest? It was not for lack of interest. For me, from about the time I went to University, as for many of my age, the First World War came to be a huge and special interest. The fiftieth anniversary of the outbreak of the War occurred in August 1964, when I was at University reading history, and old enough to understand something of the causes and consequences of the War. The anniversary was marked by an astonishing outpouring of material. There were very many excellent books that examined the War from a distance that allowed an objectivity denied to earlier studies. The atmosphere of the times, of the 'sixties, allowed and encouraged an irreverent and critical examination of the military leadership, which generally emerged badly. The new Sunday colour supplements were an ideal medium for a study of the conflict in a way that combined popular appeal and scholarship. We were soon familiar with the different types of gas mask and the detailed construction of trenches, from firestep to parados.

The wonderfully accessible and moving poetry of the War was reissued. I read Owen and Sassoon avidly, especially Sassoon, whom I researched further at Glasgow University Library, moving on to his foxhunting trilogy and then to the trilogy of his 'indoor self': *The Old Century, The Weald of Youth* and *Siegfried's Progress*. Graves and Blunden and the others followed.

My imagination was caught also by a radio programme in a series known as *Songs for the Times*. This had been assembled by

Charles Chilton, whose researches flowed from his reaction to the huge memorial at Thiepval. When it was inaugurated in July 1932 by the Prince of Wales, it was, and it still is, the largest British War Memorial in the world. It was designed by Sir Edwin Lutyens, 150 feet high and dominating the surrounding area. It is there to commemorate 73,357 British and South African men *who have no known grave* and who fell on the Somme between July 1916 and 20 March 1918. Chilton found it impossible to conceive of a conflict that could be so devastating that in one theatre of war alone and in the space of less than two years, that number of people was reduced to fragments and vapour. His reaction was to assemble a programme that juxtaposed the patriotic songs and jingoism of those at home with the plaintive and harrowing songs that the soldiers sang, and through both to interlard the poetry and prose of the war. The message that pervaded this remarkable programme which I recorded and played again and again, as my daughters were to do a generation later, was from Wilfred Owen's beautifully sharp and uncompromising *Apologia pro Poemate Meo*: 'These men are worth/ Your tears. You are not worth their merriment'.

I was not the only one whose imagination was caught by what Chilton had done: it was the germ of Joan Littlewood's *Oh, What a Lovely War*, which I managed to see in London on my way home from Oxford at the end of term. In its turn, *Oh, What a Lovely War* was the inspiration for a piece called *That'll be the Day* which was performed at the Citizens' Theatre in Glasgow for which I did the research in a University vacation. The theme of the play was to be the contrast between the promises of the politicians during wars, notably the Boer War and the First World War, with the reality of the ensuing peace. (I found that the politicians of the First World War, with only one or two exceptions, had in fact been remarkably cautious in their statements about what would follow the War.) The production, for various reasons, was not a great success, but the work I did brought me close to some aspects of the War, particularly the newspaper coverage at home, and the post-war commentary in the radical press.

The result of all this was to make me, and I think many of my contemporaries, feel close to the tragedy of the 1914–18 War, much closer to it than we felt to the Second World War, which had finished only twenty years previously. On Saturday nights we hastened back to College from the pubs of Oxford to crowd into the Junior Common Room and watch two seminal television programmes. The second was the satirical programme that so greatly influenced the mood of the times, *That Was the Week, That Was*. The first was a remarkable series, *The Great War,* that lasted for over 18 hours in total and for which Sir Michael Redgrave spoke the narrative in sombre tones. The progress or descent from the idealism of 1914 to the realities of Flanders presents an agonising disillusionment that did not really arise in the Second World War. I often dreamed of being in the trenches in these years, and I still occasionally do, although the time that has now passed since 1914 is so great that to go back as far from that date would take us to just 11 years after the Battle of Waterloo.

So why then did I never ask Ronald a single question about his brother or his brother's war? Why did I research away at second hand when I could have learned so much at first hand? I should like to think that it was considerate reticence that stopped me. I knew from my own observations as well as what Elsie had told me that Ronald found it painful to talk about Ernest. Even in his late 60s there could be a choke in his voice on one of the rare occasions when Ernest was mentioned. I had an easy and open relationship with Ronald, and it would not have been difficult to raise the subject. And there were many hooks to which I could have attached a question. An instance at random: I recall once in perhaps the 1970s when I was humming (in what Ronald had once described, uncontentiously as he thought, but rather to my surprise, as my 'tuneless, irrythmic' way) the French folk song *'Auprès de ma Blonde'*. He was struck by the melody (which therefore does not seem to have been totally tuneless) and reflected that he had not heard it for forty years. It did not need a lot of thought to realise that the arithmetic was faulty and who it was that he had last heard singing this song of the French countryside. But I said nothing. I fear that the reasons for my silence were more complicated and less altruistic than considerate. Indeed I suspect that my father might have welcomed an invitation to open his heart about the brother he still grieved. Why do we hesitate to ask our elders about the memories that will die with them? Do we feel that we put ourselves at a disadvantage that imperils our independence? Do we seek to avoid reminding them and ourselves of their mortality?

At any rate, the memories did die and the questions went unasked. But they remained in my mind, and my interest in Ernest grew as the years passed, and I became conscious that most of even my second-hand memories will die with me, and that perhaps I owed it to Ernest, who left no descendants, and to my descendants who may be no more questioning than I, to record what I knew and could find out of the uncle I never knew.

The materials I had to work with are not extensive. There are no diaries. The brown leather suitcase full of letters that I remembered so well had disappeared when I looked for it after Ronald's death. I have no doubt that he destroyed the contents and that he would feel it wrong that the private correspondence between a young officer and his parents should be open to the indiscriminate regard of third parties for whom it was never intended. I am reinforced in this view by the fact that he did retain two letters which were addressed to him and not to his parents. These he would feel he was entitled to retain – or perhaps they were simply too precious for him to destroy. Now, 85 years after the letters were written, I should have felt tempted to open and share these letters, but I respect Ronald's decision, and even if I regret the absence of the brown leather suitcase, to an extent I am glad not to face a temptation to which I should certainly have succumbed.

There are other materials to work from – a long narrative from Ernest's batman, a letter from his Commanding Officer, an invaluable scrapbook of cuttings which my secretary saved for me from one of the periodic cleansings of my Augean offices. Taken together, these materials shed light on Ernest from a variety of angles, even if no one beam illuminates him in whole. I was very fortunate also in what a search in the Public Record Office at Kew supplied. The personal files of First World War officers have only recently been opened. And what was available to open was very limited: many of the files had been destroyed by bombing in the Second World War. The enemy that had taken away these men's lives in the First World War sought to take away their memories in the Second. Only a minority survived, but fortunately the file for Ernest was part of that minority. And there are of course family traditions that I received from Elsie and from Ronald. Where these traditions conflict with written evidence, they have been amended or discarded; otherwise I have accepted them as accurate.

Without diaries and the contents of the suitcase, evidence of the internal Ernest is exiguous. What I have tried to do is to give some idea of the family, the home, the society, the culture that formed him: to recreate him, as it were, from the mould in which he was created. It seems to me that Ernest was surrounded by influences which *would* peculiarly have the capacity to form his character and personality as we are not influenced today. He was a product of Scotland at a time when the component parts of the United Kingdom had an individuality that has since been eroded by travel, communication and shared entertainment.

He was educated in the Scottish way, rigorous and demanding. Evangelical religion, and the whole way of life that went with it, was a huge part of his upbringing, and it would be impressed on him from his early days that it was his duty to develop his abilities to the full and use them for the benefit of society as well as for himself. The concept of duty was not disparaged, but reinforced in a way that we find difficult to understand, by all the apparatus of Victorian culture. The songs and poetry of the times exalt duty and self-sacrifice. Wordsworth apostrophised Duty directly, and Wordsworthian echoes have been used to link the chapters of this memoir. Lord Tennyson provided many other appropriate verses, and contemporary anthologies are full of examples. The traditions of heroism provided by stories of the Thin Red Line, the death of General Gordon, gallantry in the Zulu Wars, were cherished and never attacked. These days and these values are not ours and the change in our outlook over 85 years must be constantly remembered. These stories and poems were read by Ernest's contemporaries with real emotion. In 1960 I was sufficiently struck by the freshness and irreverence of a remark of Jonathan Miller to record it in my Commonplace Book: 'The only reasonable response to the news of the Light Brigade fiasco is, "Bloody fools"'. Today Jonathan Miller's judgement would not even be thought worth recording: that is one measure of the gap that separates us from the values that surrounded Ernest. The most famous attack on these values, Strachey's *Eminent Victorians*, was not published until 1918, and for all the reaction it provoked, it is very cautious criticism by comparison with what we expect today.

What I think emerges from the mould is an understated hero. He did nothing that was exceptional for a man in his situation, and he received no award for gallantry; but that he was a hero seems to me incontestable. He pressed forward to the service of his country. He was ready to sacrifice himself for his ideals, and his idealism was never compromised by cynicism. His gallantry on the field of battle was exemplary. He laid down his life for those he loved.

The fact that there were so many others who did as much makes it more and not less important to remember him. Each memory that is lost diminishes the scale of what they did.

2

The Elements of Feeling and of Thought

ERNEST IN HIS LANDSCAPE

Ernest was very much a product of Paisley and Renfrewshire, but his roots, both paternal and maternal, were in Ayrshire. The Reids can be traced back to Kilwinning in that county in the middle of the seventeenth century, in or near the hamlet of Reidstoun. Little biographical information is available until we reach John Reid of Fairlie Boag, Kilwinning. He was born in 1753 and had a small farm. His son, William, was born in 1788 and it was he who made the move from Ayrshire to Paisley.

He moved to a town of about 5,000 people which had a long history. There is a local tradition that there were two Roman forts where Paisley is, but it is now accepted that the habitation which Ptolemy called Vanduara is not on its site, despite claims to the contrary. The earliest historical record of what is now the town is the establishment there in the twelfth century of a Cluniac Monastery by Walter Fitzallan, who had been given lands in Renfrewshire by David I. The monastery was to become Paisley Abbey, capable of supporting itself because it was situated on good agricultural land close to the River Cart. There was already a flour mill in the nearby village of Seedhill, now part of Paisley, which was gifted to the Abbey, and the site was of some importance in medieval times. It was on the King's highway at the point where it crossed the Cart by the Paisley or Seedhill ford, and on the route, through what is called the Lochwinnoch Gap, to the rich agricultural lands of Ayrshire, and the coast.

Through the middle ages and till the seventeenth or eighteenth centuries, Paisley remained a quiet market town, flourishing, at least until the Reformation, because of the Abbey. The agricultural richness of the area which had attracted Fitzallan to the location in the first place continued to generate prosperity, and the monks stimulated and encouraged good husbandry. James IV made the village of Paisley a royal burgh in 1488.

What radically changed the economy of the town was the establishment of an important textile industry – or rather a series of textile industries: there was a succession of rises and declines of a variety of enterprises. Weaving had been an important occupation in the town from an early point: in the Poll Tax Roll for Renfrewshire for 1695, the weavers outnumbered all other tradesmen. By the early eighteenth century, Paisley was an established regional centre for textiles and its fabrics were well known in England as well as in Scotland. Initially rough linens and mixed fabrics were manufactured, but from this developed the manufacture of linen yarn, and this was to be the basis of the town's prosperity throughout the eighteenth century.

As that century approaches, and with it the Age of Enlightenment, it is worth looking for a moment at an extraordinary incident which sheds light on the persistence of medieval ideas into modern times, and which was eventually to have an important effect on the local textile industry. On 30 December 1696, at a meeting of Paisley Presbytery, the minister of Erskine reported the bewitching of Christian Shaw, the daughter of the Laird of Bargarran. Christian was in her early teens. She was suffering from wild convulsions, with rolling eyes and frothing mouth. She had episodes of blindness and could be deaf and mute. When she vomited she threw up feathers, straw, hay, rags, bones, coal, stones and candles. The doctors said that she was bewitched.

The case was reported to the Privy Council in Edinburgh and Commissioners were appointed to deal with the matter. Arrests were carried out throughout the whole county of Renfrew in a frenzy that illustrates the aptness of the metaphor, 'witchhunt'. Christian herself accused some people directly, including a servant girl who had said to her, 'The devil harl [take] your soul to hell'. Some were named by others of the accused.

'Prickers', professional witch identifiers, were called in. The accused men and women were stripped and their bodies searched with a large needle. If a spot were found where the prick of the needle was not felt and there was no bleeding, that was clear evidence that the devil's fingers had touched the warlock or witch.

These prickers, remember (and the Commissioners, of whom there were 17, educated men of consequence, including Lord Blantyre, Sir John Maxwell of Pollok, Sir John Shaw of Greenock and William Cunningham of Craigends), were contemporaries of Locke and Newton. The Privy Council was composed of even more substantial men, sophisticated and frequently educated in Europe as well as in Scotland. But within a generation of the Age of Enlightenment, when Gibbon was to speak of the brave light of philosophy breaking in from Scotland, they sent for the prickers.

Twenty-one men and women were put on trial in the Tolbooth of Paisley before the King's Commissioners in May 1697. Three men and four women were convicted and were condemned to be throttled and burned on the Gallow Green on 10 June of that year. One of the men hanged himself in his cell, and it was understood that the devil had been impatient for his soul, and had strangled the man himself.

The remaining six were taken to the Gallow Green. Stakes had been driven into the ground and one was chained to each stake. The hangman passed along the line strangling each person with a rope. Then kindling dipped in tar was piled around the victims, whose bodies were burnt.

Local legend says that the remains of the bodies were buried at the point where George Street and Maxwellton Street cross. There is there a horseshoe embedded in a causey stone, which was left in place in recent years when all the other causey stones were lifted. It is said that this marks the place where the witches and warlocks were burned and that the horseshoe keeps their spirits down.

There was a coda to the story in the nineteenth century when a local man known as Pate the Pirate drunkenly prised the horse-shoe out of the stone. Immediately there was an epidemic of suicides, and weavers hanged themselves all over the town. Pate sobered up and confessed what he had done: the horseshoe was replaced and at once the suicides stopped.

The connection between this story of witches and the textile industry is Christian Shaw. She recovered completely. In 1718 she married the parish minister of Kilmaurs. He died after only three years and she then set off with her mother to explore the Low Countries, where she became interested in the thread industry which Holland had more or less monopolised. She and her mother studied the operations in detail and smuggled apparatus and plans home, where they set up a factory at Bargarran. Christian proved a very capable businesswoman and her enterprise flourished remarkably, and so this woman, whose youth resembles something from the early Middle Ages, ends up as an integral part of the Industrial Revolution. The girl who starts off being remembered for flying around her room is finally 'regarded as a founder of the sewing thread industry'.

By 1789 that industry employed no less than 4,800 workers. Alongside the production of thread, other textile industries came and went. Linen gave way to silk. In 1766, 855 looms produced linen and 702 silk; by 1773 only 557 looms were producing linen and 876 were producing silk. Paisley was the main centre for the production of silk in Britain for several years but, typically of the rise and fall of these textile trades, silk manufacture began to decline as early as 1790, and by 1812 there was no silk production in the town.

For a time cotton took its place, and in the nineteenth century shawls with the so-called pine pattern design, 'the Paisley pattern', had become a signature Paisley product. But the garment was essentially a fashion item and its popularity faded, despite Queen Victoria's attempt to encourage it by wearing the shawl. By 1882 there were fewer than 1,000 weavers in Paisley and there were not 50 left by 1910.

More enduring was the production of cotton thread. It became mechanised and was extremely important to Paisley. In the mid-nineteenth century there were 45 firms in Paisley producing thread, but much the most important businesses were those run by two families: the Coats and the Clarks. These families were generous benefactors, but ruthless business people. They became linked by marriage and soon controlled the whole of the local industry, forcing every competing firm in the town out of business. They bought up those who would sell at premium prices; the others were undercut and driven into liquidation. These monopolist techniques were applied on almost every continent, so that by 1910 Paisley was regarded as the thread capital of the world; and over 10,000 were employed in Paisley itself. The Coats/Clark nexus was an empire of mills, dominating and impressive buildings, built on a palatial scale and scattered around the world, sending their profits back to Renfrewshire.

The Clark and Coats families were large ones, and many people could boast a connection with them, as indeed could the Reids. The grandest members of the clan were very grand indeed. Titles were conferred on them, they became the friends of Edward VII and George V and they distanced themselves as much as they could from the source of their mercantile fortunes. Others were not so grand. The clan was for convenience divided into the Greatcoats and the Petticoats. The Reids' connection was with the Petticoats.

Paisley was on the wrong side of Scotland for access to the trade routes to Europe, but by the nineteenth century, trade to the west had become at least as important as that to mainland Europe. Until the Clyde was dredged as far as Glasgow, ships from the Americas had to berth at Port Glasgow, at the mouth of the Clyde, and Paisley was on the route from the port to Glasgow itself. Indeed there was a scheme late in the century to dredge the Cart, Paisley's tributary of the Clyde, which would have benefited Paisley at Glasgow's expense. The project was never completed and it rendered the burgh bankrupt for many years.

This was not the only time when things were difficult for Paisley: there was a major recession in the town as in many other parts of Britain in the 1840s. But by and large Paisley benefited from the Industrial Revolution. It was the availability of water that had attracted Walter Fitzallan in the first place, and when the Industrial Revolution, which came to the West of Scotland early, reached Renfrewshire, the Cart and its tributaries supported innumerable small manufacturers.

William, the first of the Reids for whom we have significant biographical material, was attracted to the town by these commercial stirrings. His career is an elegant demonstration of the Industrial Revolution in practice. He moved from Ayrshire, where the economic activities were largely agriculture and fishing, to the nascent industrialisation of Paisley. He is described initially as having the rural occupation of blacksmith; but in a significant change he emerges in later documents as an 'iron boat builder'. He was to be involved in a quintessential phenomenon of the early Industrial Revolution, the network of canals that spread over Britain before their eclipse by the railways. He seized the opportunity that was created by a plan for a canal to run from Glasgow, through Paisley, to the Ayrshire coast. After a survey (the cost of which was subsidised by Paisley Town Council to the extent of £5), and an Act of Parliament, construction of the canal began in 1807 and the section from Paisley to Johnstone was opened on 6 November 1810. A year later the section between Paisley and Glasgow was completed.

At first it took two hours to cover the seven miles from Paisley to Glasgow and the canal could not compete with coaches; but an advance was made in 1836 which was crucial for the industry and for William, when the heavy old boats were taken off and light boats made of iron were introduced. They were drawn by two trotting horses travelling at 10 miles an hour and there were stables at intervals of four miles along the canal bank where the horses were changed, as the writer Alexander Smith described:

The drag-rope was loosened, and the long boat with its white awning, under which the people sat, came alongside the wooden wharf with a bump. Parcels were tossed out, parcels were tossed in; passengers stepped carefully in and disappeared under the awning; passengers emerged from the awning and stepped carefully out.

In 1836 the canal carried 423,186 passengers in its 'gig-boats'. The charge was considerable for the time: ninepence for cabin or sixpence for steerage. Separate freight boats carried 67,305 tons of luggage. The passenger boats left Paisley and Glasgow every hour throughout the day.

For a brief period William Reid must have done very well indeed. It *was* only brief, because the year after the light boats were introduced, the first railway was opened between Paisley and Renfrew and by 1840 there were two railway lines between Glasgow and the coast, each of which passed through Paisley. The canal continued in use, however, and it was only in 1882 that it disappeared, when it was bought by the Glasgow & South Western Railway Company, who used its bed for a railway track.

William's firm, Reid & Hannah, was commissioned to create the iron ships out of sheet-iron. What he had to build was like an extraordinary, elongated racing hull, 70 feet long by 4 feet 9 inches wide. The similarity to a canoe was noted. The hulls were carried from his yard at Orr Square to the canal and then towed to Johnstone where they were fitted out. The fittings included partitions between the first- and second-class accommodation which gave the hull its rigidity. Later a special wagon was made to take the boats from Reid & Hannah's workshop to the fitting-out timber yard. It might have been simpler to build the boats beside the water: maybe William could see that the sun in which he was making his hay would not shine for long.

The main figure in the canal company was William Houston of Johnstone. He noticed that as business developed for Reid & Hannah, with other canals looking for iron boats from them,

William Reid had sub-contracted some of the work to another Paisley firm for fitting out. By this time William was manufacturing boats for all parts of Britain. Houston, as a Johnstone landowner, resented the fact that the fitting out was being diverted to a Paisley firm and he encouraged the establishment of another iron boat builder in his burgh. The two firms seem to have been able to exist side by side, and each of them manufactured boats that were used throughout Britain and further afield. William supplied the boats for the Aberdeen Canal, the Duke of Bridgewater's Canal and the Paddington Canal, and he sent boats to France, South America and Ireland.

But the period of manufacturing for the Paisley canal itself was brief. Critically, the canal never reached the coast or went further west than Johnstone. And competition with the railway companies was brisk and short-lived: by 1843 the canal company agreed to sell them its fast boats and limit itself to slow-going freight. In return the railways carried no substantial freight between Glasgow and Paisley and made an annual payment to the canal company to compensate it for lost business.

In my diningroom are portraits of William and his wife Janet Macarthur (an example of a weakness of Reids for Janets that is reflected in the family tree for centuries and continues today). His prosperity is confirmed by the fact that he had oil portraits done of himself and his wife, and by the fact that she came from a substantial local family. His portrait is executed with skill and conveys authority, shrewdness and some humour. He is holding a document which may well be a plan for one of his iron ships. Janet is attractive and dignified. There is again perhaps the tiniest of smiles about her mouth, but she gives little away.

William died in 1854. He had eight children including James, Ernest's grandfather, who was born in 1812. James's career illustrates the twists and turns of the Paisley economy in the nineteenth century. He was first a shawl manufacturer. Then he was a clerk in a coal business, and latterly he was a wood turner. The first occupation may have been profitable at first, but would not be so for long. Not much can be said about his second choice of career. The third could have been a very remunerative niche, presumably supplying bobbins to the fast-growing thread mills. He married Jessie Fulton in 1858. At that time he lived at 32 Oakshaw Street, Paisley, which was a good address in the oldest part of Paisley, the spine of hill that dominates the centre of the town and is one of the putative sites of the Roman Vanduara. By the time his son, Tom, was getting married, James had moved to 48 Causeyside Street which Ronald was to buy 65 years later, as the office for his legal practice. He bought the property unaware of the family connection which he discovered only shortly before his death. The building was originally a rather attractive townhouse, with fairly extensive accommodation, including several rooms for servants. It is marked externally by a pair of Ionic pillars surmounted by a classical tympanum, and internally was distinguished by some excellent plasterwork. That, along with most of the other marks of architectural distinction, has been, I have to admit, destroyed by father and son as we put commercial necessities above aesthetic values.

3

Still and Serious Thought

THE PARENTAL HOME

James died in 1887. He, like his father, had eight children, including Ernest's father Tom, who was born in 1858.

Tom was almost certainly educated at Paisley Grammar School. He then became a lawyer. As was not uncommon in those days, he did not matriculate at Glasgow University, but attended classes there early every morning, before spending the rest of a long day in a solicitors' office. The late afternoon might involve a return to the University, and the evening would be spent working on the day's lecture notes. It was a discipline to which my father was in turn to submit, and from which I, in the more liberal but perhaps less effective mode of legal education in the 1960s, was glad to have been spared. He then sat, and qualified as a solicitor by passing, examinations set by the Scottish Law Agents' Society.

Family tradition says that he put up his professional brass plate and started to practise law for the first time at the age of 21. In fact there is documentation that suggests that he had done so even before he reached the age of majority and that he was practising in Paisley as early as 1878. But in 1882 his diaries indicate that he was working for another solicitor, David Semple, so it appears he moved from self-employment to employment, and reasonably well paid employment for a very young lawyer with little experience: he was receiving a salary of £100 a year, or about £10,000 a year in today's money. Mr Semple however declined in 1882 to give him an increase and Tom left him at the end of May, striking off on his own for good. As firms did in those days, he moved from place to place in Paisley, when leases became available and fell in. He practised first on his own and then in partnership with a Mr McKenzie. This did not last long and he soon entered into a partnership with John Donaldson which was to last, under the firm name of T. F. Reid & Donaldson, until he retired. Initially he practised only in Paisley, but latterly he had offices in both Glasgow and Paisley. He worked hard and had amongst his clients some builders. There was much for them to do. At the end of the nineteenth century and beginning of the twentieth there was an enormous amount of building going on in the West of Scotland. Particularly in the years from 1890 to 1909 (after which Lloyd George's Budget of that year, with its 20% tax on the increment value of property, put a sudden end to speculative building), the whole landscape changed, as towns expanded and as the older cores of towns and cities were wholly rebuilt. Until this outbreak of building, conditions, bad enough in Glasgow and other industrial towns in the area, were even worse in Paisley: many of the houses were still thatched in straw, despite bye-laws that forbade such roofing because of the fire danger. Most were single-storey. The rooms were poorly lit. The ceilings were low and the walls were damp, as rain seeped through the roof. Beds were built into unventilated recesses. Despite the fact that Paisley was the first town in the world to have a filtered water supply, disease was rife well into the nineteenth century, with repeated outbreaks of typhus, enteric fever, smallpox, scarlet fever and diphtheria. There were outbreaks of cholera in 1832 and 1835. Of the eight principal towns in Scotland in 1861, Paisley had the lowest number of rooms in proportion to population. In the 1870s the town council did begin to remove older properties to widen the streets, but they did so without ensuring that there was alternative accommodation for those evicted: they further overcrowded the other old areas. By 1890 more than 31% of all families still lived in houses consisting of just one room.

But these were the facts of life and death in nineteenth-century Scotland. What would strike Tom in his 20s was the huge improvement in these figures and the vast change that he could see going on around him in the town. From a population of about 60,000 in 1830 Paisley had grown to about 80,000 by the end of the century. In a progress report of Paisley Corporation in 1902 it was claimed that the real progress of Paisley had taken place during the previous thirty years. It was the fifth biggest town in Scotland. One councillor boasted that 'Paisley is esteemed the richest town in the kingdom'. Although the obverse of this dynamic growth was that many people still lived in old, decaying property and festering slums, what was noticeable was how fast this was changing. Writing in 1909, the Rev. Dr W. M. Metcalfe in his history of the town listed the changes that had taken place in the previous sixty years:

> The ancient village of Paisley and Seedhill, the Fuller's Mill, and the school that were once there have disappeared. Causeyside Street has been altered out of all recognition, the Corsehouse in front of which once stood the Cross of St Ninian has been pulled down. Gordon's Loan, along which traffic was once led to the Black Ford, is now unrecognisable; Prussia Street, Orchard Street and New Street have ceased to be what they were; the High Street has in part been widened and lined with new and handsome buildings; Well-meadow and Broomlands are marked down for alterations similar to those effected in the High Street; and in the Broomlands some of the proposed alterations have already been made. The part west of Dyers Wynd from Gilmour Street to Moss Street has been demolished, and the space at the Cross has thus been made double the size of what it used to be.

Dr Metcalfe did not know how suddenly the Budget of the same year as his history would put a stop to this building pro-gramme: in Glasgow in 1902 the Dean of Guild Court passed linings (planning permissions) for 4,600 houses of one, two or three apartments. In 1910 there were only 250. For the next 35 years, as a consequence of the Budget and the Scottish rating system, practically no houses were built for rent in the West of Scotland. The changes that Dr Metcalfe described were of more than academic interest to Tom. As he prospered, he was able to lend money to some of his builder clients, to help finance their activities. In a relationship that would be frowned on by the Law Society of Scotland today, he thus gained not only interest on the capital he advanced, but also valuable conveyancing business.

For some time this symbiotic relationship worked greatly to his advantage, as well as that of his clients, and the young solicitor prospered. Ultimately, however, the arrangement was to backfire on him, when one or more clients defaulted. The consequences do not appear to have affected his lifestyle significantly, but Ronald spoke of it as an experience that impressed him. After what had been a fairly affluent way of life, he was conscious of the relative indignity of having to adapt expenditure to a reduced income. The experience must have been a largely relative matter and cannot have been long-lasting, but the recollection of the experience was to affect his own choice of career.

The genes of the Reids ensured that my wife, like that of William and of so many others, was a Janet. Her paternal grandfather, Hugh McPherson, was, as it happens, also a Paisley man, born in 1870, in a single-storey thatched cottage like those that Tom saw pulled down daily. His birth falls roughly halfway between those of Tom and Ernest, and thus the memories of Paisley that he committed to paper in his old age are a valuable record of what must have been familiar to both of them. Beyond that, he was a remarkable man in his own right, and his career is an example of the response of a young Scot to the influences which informed the lives of the time. This response was expressed for him in terms of service to the State and duty to the Empire.

Hugh's diaries provide glimpses of the society and surroundings, not greatly changed, in which Ernest, 27 years his junior, would grow up. Echoes and similarities resonate between the physical and moral frameworks of their early lives.

There is one early difference between them. Tom and Ernest were members of households in which alcohol was unknown; Hugh, on his own account, was brought up in a home where habits were rather different. Indeed, but for that we would know much less about him, for part of his purpose in writing *Notes* for his children appears to have been to alert them to what he had seen happen to his father, who 'unfortunately . . . gradually gave way to habits of intemperance and thereby wrecked his business career and shortened his life'. He lists other members of his family whose lives were affected by a similar affliction and explains that, 'I have mentioned this fatal weakness . . . as a caution to my children and children's children, not because I think the weakness is hereditary, but because it is necessary to be on guard against the family pre-disposition', a predisposition with which my children unkindly tease their mother by referring to it as 'the Curse of the McPhersons'.

The incidence of intemperance was probably no higher in the McPhersons' family than in many other families of that time in the West of Scotland, but for Hugh, as for Tom, life was far too important a gift to be shortened or sabotaged by an excessive consumption of alcohol. From his *Notes*, Hugh emerges as in many ways similar to what we know of Ernest: highminded but not without a sense of humour, not serious so much as *sérieux;* he combined high principles with a worldly ambition to which his principles were not sacrificed. Beginning from humbler origins than Ernest, but in a longer life which happily was not cut short by war, he achieved great success in the Indian Civil Service, retiring to Scotland in 1925 as Sir Hugh McPherson, a Knight Commander of the Indian Empire, Acting Governor of Bihar and Orissa, laden with honours. In his retirement he exercised his body by climbing the Scottish mountains – or those of wherever else he happened to be – and his mind by working on Greek and Latin translations with Janet's maternal grandfather, a retired headmaster.

Hugh was able to say that the local histories which claimed that the production of the Paisley shawl had ceased altogether by 1870 were not entirely accurate:

> In my schoolboy days I often used to watch hand-loom weavers at work on harness shawls. They plied their craft in workrooms containing half a dozen or more looms, forming the ground floors of residential houses. They were a highly intelligent class, taking the keenest interest in politics and religion, which they used to discuss in the intervals of their work.

Most of his family belonged to this weaving community. In the same families, some members would be actual weavers, whereas others were middlemen, or manufacturers, who financed their poorer relatives and sold their products in the shawl market. Both his grandfathers belonged to the former class, although other family members were of what he called 'the more enterprising type'. But by the time Hugh's father was ready to go to work, the handloom industry was falling into decay and he was apprenticed to a brick-building firm of which in time he became manager, supervising a considerable number of bricklayers and labourers. He went on to take over the business and in his son's view 'might have lived to attain high commercial success' but for the family predisposition.

At the age of five, Hugh began to attend the infant classes of George Street School, near his home at Castle Street and 'run by a spinster dame called Miss Smith. I can still remember her skeletal, rugged features which veiled a kind heart. The head–master of this school was John Taylor, a large, florid man and a strict disciplinarian whose tawse [or leather belt] was a terror to his pupils'.

Hugh and Ernest were moulded by the same secondary education. In the summer of 1882, when he was 12 years old, Hugh won a Cochran scholarship, which was tenable for four years at Paisley Grammar School, and was worth £12 a year, covering the cost of fees and class books. 'This,' he wrote, 'was the turning point in my life history, for it gave me access to the best secondary education in Paisley and opened the way to Glasgow University.' He makes no secret of the fact that he worked hard and set out to excel: 'I had a tough struggle in my first year at the Grammar School for top place in the classes with John Gibb of Gladstone Farm, but I beat him and in three years' time I became the acknowledged Head of the school, winning all the first and special prizes and getting the class medals'.

The rigours of Scottish education at that time are reflected in the way in which he ended his last summer term, in 1886:

We had for our showpiece a reproduction in miniature of the Home Rule Debate, which was then convulsing Parliament and the country. We senior scholars spouted abridged editions of the parliamentary speeches of the principal protagonists. I took the part of Mr Gladstone, the Prime Minister and G.O.M., and I still remember his closing words. After referring to the parallel of Canada and the insistent demand of the Irish Nation for autonomous government, he ended, 'Think well, think wisely, think not for the moment but for the years that are to come, before you regret that demand.'

The culture of Paisley Grammar School, as he experienced it, was the same, demanding and uncompromising, when Ernest followed him there. Its aim was unashamedly élitist, if that de-scribes the objective of fitting its ablest pupils for entry to University and the professions. Both Hugh and Ernest went from Paisley Grammar School to Glasgow University by way of competitive scholarships. In the summer of 1886 Hugh sat the Preliminary (or entrance) examination and Bursary Competition of Glasgow University at which, he allowed himself to recall,

several hundred pupils from Glasgow High Schools and West Country Grammar Schools and Academies competed. I had the thrill of my life when I found my name at the top of the list of successful candidates on going in one morning with fellow students from Paisley to see the results of the examination. This success gave me the John Clark Mile-End Bursary, worth £40 a year for four years. The Grammar School celebrated my success with a one day holiday.

At Glasgow University he decided where his career was to be. At one time he had expected to go into the church, 'a common goal of Scottish students who were ambitious to "wag their heads in the pulpit" '. Medicine also appealed, but had to be ruled out on the grounds of expense. He considered business, and it is informative that here his interest lay not in the accumulation of wealth, but in the extension of the principles of the co-operative movement which he thought could be applied to industry, developing his father's building business on lines of co-partnership between capital and labour. In the event he was encouraged by family friends to make his career in the Indian Civil Service, and duty and service took him to the sub-continent as they were to take Ernest to the Western Front.

His passage to India lay partly through the London University matriculation exam (in which he came out third of 940 candidates) and partly via a Snell exhibition to Balliol, a route which took so many able and ambitious young Scots to Oxford and success in the wider world.

By the time he went to Oxford he had secured sufficient scholarships and bursaries to be assured of a comfortable income of £313 a year (in excess of £15,500 today). He was able to reflect with understandable pride that, 'My education had cost my parents nothing from the age of 12 and I was now in a position to help them and my brothers and sister at home'.

He was to regard his years at Balliol as among the most pleasant years of his life. He mixed with a diverse body of undergraduates, whose only common features were considerable ability and a quite remarkable desire, which was generally fulfilled, for worldly success. This was Balliol under Jowett at its apogee, a forcing house for men of capacity who would work hard and who would make an indelible imprint on the professions and politics and administration of late-Victorian Britain and its Empire. Hugh must have come from a distinctly less elevated social background than most of his contemporaries, but his biographical *Notes*, like other accounts of the College at this period, do not suggest that he felt or would feel abashed: he was part of a freemasonry of ability, in which (within limits) social origins were not of significance:

> Life at Oxford 50 years ago [he wrote in the 1940s] was a pleasant business, work being varied agreeably with play. Our forenoons were generally devoted to lectures, our afternoons to exercise, followed by tea, our evenings to Hall, conversation, and, for the industrious, study. One began the day with a cold bath (in a shallow zinc tub), followed or preceded by Chapel. Breakfast was brought to our rooms by the Scouts. I did not like the mess produced from the Buttery as porridge and after the first term, brought down my own oatmeal from Scotland and made my own.

Hugh manages to make the régime sound relaxed, when he describes students meeting in each other's rooms for tea or coffee after Hall and discussing 'every subject under the sun – politics, religion, economics – with all the assurance of the undergraduate outlook'. But the relaxation is relative only to the perhaps more joyless days he had known in Scotland. It is evident that a great deal of hard work went on as well, as he later admits. In addition to hard work, there was some very hard exercise – rowing, skating and the incredibly long walks that seem to have been a feature of Oxford life in those days. Hugh walked the 55 miles from London to Oxford with one friend. In the summer term he took walks of 20 or 30 miles around Oxford with others. On another occasion there was a walking tour from Oxford to Birkenhead through Derbyshire. A second walk from London to Oxford he appears to have regarded as a particular achievement. He and a friend left Marble Arch at 3 a.m. and had breakfast at Uxbridge. His friend's shoes gave out and had to be replaced. The new shoes were so painful that the friend had to abandon the journey some 42 miles out from London, finding 'a passing waggoner to take him to the nearest railway station'. Hugh suffered agonies from his knees on the last lap, arriving in Hall about 8 p.m. after '17 hours on the journey, of which 14 was spent walking, making an average for the 55 miles of four miles *per* hour'. He admits that it took him three or four days to recover.

Hugh enumerates his contemporaries and their achievements in a list which is far too extensive to repeat here, but which no Oxford or Cambridge college nowadays or, I would suggest, any one university could surpass. The achievement was Jowett's, and that of some of the Fellows whom he had assembled. One of Hugh's contemporaries was Francis ('Sligger') Urquhart, who was appointed Dean of the College in 1918. He became a cult figure, hugely influential on a generation of Oxonians, and referred to in many autobiographies. He gathered round him young undergraduates whom he identified as 'winners', encouraged them, and brought them on – not for material reward, but, it would appear, simply for the sake of enjoying the warmth that their achievements reflected on him. Much of his encouragement was given at the chalet in Switzerland where his famously spartan reading parties took place, and Hugh met him again at St Gervais-les-Bains in 1930.

Jowett himself was over 70 when Hugh went up to Balliol. Hugh describes his snow-white hair and cherubic countenance. He had been a Fellow of the College since 1835 and Master since 1870. Hugh notes his abrupt, laconic mode of speech and his uncompromising failure to break his silence when he took freshmen, as he did, on long walks. Hugh did not have many meetings with Jowett, although he was invited to coffee with him in his rooms after Hall on one or two occasions. He describes one result of Jowett's methods: the great array of eminent men, his 'old boys', who came frequently as guests to the High Table or the Balliol Concerts.

And in a typical piece of Balliol networking, the Master gave Hugh, when he went off from Oxford to India, and leaves this narrative, a letter of introduction to the Viceroy, Lord Lansdowne.

The contrast between the beginnings of Hugh's life in the single-storey thatched house in Castle Street and the imperial splendour of the Governor's palace in which his career ended has always struck me as remarkable and romantic: an example of the way in which, despite all the rigidity of the Victorian class and hierarchical system, a young man of ability, with very real determination, could grasp glittering prizes. Castle Street was the sort of house that generally disappeared before the end of the nineteenth century: in fact it remained, though with its thatched roof replaced by slates, until the 1970s. The McPhersons moved in 1881 or 1882 to a new house. Hugh's father had acquired a vacant parcel of ground, partly by inheritance and partly by purchase. Here, after evicting a squatter, he built, largely with his own hands, one of the new dwellings which were supplanting the old cottages. The building of this house was very much a demonstration of the transformation of the face of Paisley which was to accelerate in the coming years, as it was the first of the new buildings in a line of thatched cottages, a symbol of change.

The building epidemic of these twenty years was sustained because it fulfilled two social needs. First, it replaced the terrible slums that had existed as a rebuke to nineteenth-century Scotland. Secondly, it provided a means of investment for a *rentier* class who built in order to receive rent, or sold in such a way that they received both a capital payment plus an ongoing income by way of ground rents, known in Scotland as feu duties or ground annuals.

What they built in this outburst of creativity was ultimately allowed to deteriorate until it too composed slums and was either demolished or restored and refurbished in the last third of the twentieth century. But the houses and flats that went up were for the most part of very high quality with considerable architectural merits and both internal and external decoration and detail that frequently reflect the *art nouveau* tradition which was flourishing in Glasgow at that time.

For there was indeed a real buzz in the West of Scotland. Glasgow was proud to be 'the second city of the Empire'. We may now be aware that the British economy was at that very time being overtaken by those of Germany and the United States, but few people were conscious of the fact and they would certainly not have seen it as an inexorable reverse even if they had been aware of it. What they did see was Britain at the peak of her imperial power, and at home material improvements on a scale that had never been known before. It was not difficult to believe in progress as people saw industry achieving technological innovations daily, great buildings and public works appearing all round them, sanitation and public health moving from third-world to modern conditions within a single generation. Meanwhile culture was not being forgotten. Glasgow had built its huge Kelvingrove Museum and Art Gallery and the world came to its International Exhibition in 1901. People's palaces were being erected everywhere. In Paisley the munificence of the thread families gave the town an elegant museum and art gallery and a fine town hall with its reading room.

In those days, as now, Paisley people tended to emphasise the independence of their town from Glasgow and point to its long history. It is interesting, however, that in a speech which Tom made in Paisley Sheriff Court in 1917 in his capacity as Dean of the Faculty of Procurators, or solicitors, in Paisley, he was proud to refer to Paisley as 'this western suburb of the second city of the Empire'.

Indeed Paisley was linked, as never before, to that second city. As well as the railways which joined Glasgow and Paisley by their two lines, a tramway had been built in 1885 and was electrified in 1904. The lines went not just to Paisley but on to Johnstone, Kilbarchan, Renfrew and Barrhead. One could travel easily to and from Glasgow and the other outlying towns and indeed within the burgh of Paisley itself. There were no fewer than five railway stations in the town, making it easy to reach Glasgow or further afield from any part of Paisley. Competition between the railway companies was matched by competition between the same companies on the water. From each of the piers on the extensive Clyde estuary the railway company steamers raced in a flotilla of craft that crossed and recrossed the Firth to connect the villages and towns with each other and with Glasgow. Sober and bowler-hatted businessmen would start their working day with an exhilarating race across the water, throwing their *Glasgow Herald*s in the air to encourage their steamer's efforts against its rival's. Communication was facilitated by a postal service which was much more extensive than it is today. There were several collections and deliveries in the course of the day, so that it was perfectly possible to send a letter and receive a reply within a single day. By the end of the nineteenth century, businesses, if not private houses, were often linked by telephone.

This was the physical background against which the young Tom was practising and prospering. By the time he was 28 he felt sufficiently established to embark on matrimony. His response to the stirrings of his heart was not romantic: he made a short-list of suitable brides. No doubt other young men have done that, but it was not tactful to tell the bride he had selected that he had chosen her because her name was top of a list. If that was an inauspicious way to embark on matrimony, it was in fact a very happy marriage which he made with Annie Craig. Annie was from Saltcoats in Ayrshire and was related to Tom. He comes across as a sober and serious young man, but he wisely chose a bride who had a sense of humour. She was amused by Tom's confession of how she had been chosen, and was no less amused a year after their marriage. She then said to Tom, 'We have been married now a twelve-month. Is there anything that I could do to be a better wife for you?' She had expected him to deny such a possibility, but instead he gave some careful thought to the question and then said that he would indeed be pleased if she would rise rather earlier in the mornings.

Annie's father was a Master Mariner as had been others of her ancestors. One, perhaps her father, had lost money on I think not one, but two, occasions when ships were lost at sea – uninsured, because, according to a view that was by this time unusual, to insure was regarded as interfering with God's plans. I have a letter

43

which was brought out of Paris by balloon during the siege of 1870. It is from a Scottish family who are immured in the city, having been brought to France by Captain Craig. The seafaring tradition goes further back than that, and one ancestor is said to have been held a prisoner of the French during the Napoleonic war. Family tradition says that such were the privations of captivity that the rice which formed his diet was counted out, grain by grain.

Unusually, Tom and Annie spent their honeymoon in Norway, travelling from place to place as early backpackers. They were adventurous in their holidays, at least in the early years, before their family arrived.

Annie came, like Tom, from a very religious background, where Sundays were taken up by church services. She was human enough however to tell Elsie that the great interest amongst the young girls of Saltcoats was always in a new minister, and whether he might be handsome and unattached. She confided, too, that 'The Reids don't show their feelings'. There was a certain unworldliness amongst them. There were three 'saintly' aunts by whom Ronald was discomfited on one occasion. He said something to them about 'keelie boys':

'And what are keelie boys, Ronald?'
'Boys who don't wear shoes.'
'And if your father did not have enough money to buy shoes for you, would you be a keelie boy, Ronald?'

The questions were well meant. They left an impression on the little boy for the rest of his life. A family letter of the time refers to an aunt as having being spoken of 'reverently as a very good saintly woman'. Annie is quoted in the same letter as having heard of this ancestor being 'such a very sincerely spiritual woman'. Another 'aunt had a desire for her family to be religious and somehow she got her three eldest daughters married to good men'. This talk was not cant. Religion and morality were important in the lives of people at this time to an extent we find difficult to understand. A sincerity and a seriousness that did not exclude a sense of humour informed at least certain sections of society to a remarkable degree.

We know quite a lot about Tom's daily life from three of his diaries which remain extant for the years 1882, 1888 and 1889. The first covers the year in which he finally started in practice on his own account and the other two are the very early years of his marriage. They are fascinating documents. They contain detailed accounts of his expenditure month by month, and enormously detailed records of his activities every day, from morning to night. He does not perform a Gladstonian moral audit at the end of each year; but he is clearly accounting, to himself at least, for his stewardship of his talents. There is no place in the diaries for humour, but there is all the same something enormously exhilarating in their vigour, their moral purpose and their earnestness.

The picture they reveal is of a way of life that is essentially Victorian – and indeed photographs of Tom, both as a young man and towards the end of his life, reveal him bearded and dignified, in a cutaway jacket and wing collar. Ronald's oldest friend, Jimmy Thomson, who will appear later in this narrative, lived on into his nineties. In the nineties of his century and of his life, I asked him what he remembered of Tom and Annie. He said that Tom had always seemed an elderly man at the time he knew him, friendly ('Hello, James,' he would greet Jimmy), and always smartly dressed, in a frocksuit in summer, as he walked to his office, then in Moss Street. Annie always felt a little sorry for Jimmy, whom she thought a little neglected by his stepmother, and she clearly had been a motherly figure to him.

The diaries reveal much hard work; but though the hours are long, they are not regulated in these years by the need to be available on a telephone. There is much coming and going to and from the office in the course of the day. Tom was an early user of a wax cylinder dictating machine, and was able to record dictation when his letters were not written in his own hand. Life greatly involved the church, and all its various activities. The church was Victoria Place Baptist Church, and not the huge 'Baptist Cathedral' designed by Hippolyte Blanc and given to the town by the Coats family. There are politics: Tom was, naturally, an enthusiastic Liberal. At some stage in his life he acted as an agent in parliamentary elections. There is study (in areas that are surprising, such as engineering) and diligent self-improvement. The day is filled with activities, some of them certainly pleasurable, but none frivolous. The cause of temperance is furthered. Contact with friends and a large family is carefully nurtured. In these years of schisms and dissension before the 1925 Church of Scotland Act, Scots cannot be distinguished from other Scots on the basis of being non-conformist, but Tom, like many of his countrymen, had that entirely honourable combination of commercial sense and genuine spiritual concern which is to be found also amongst English non-conformists of the period.

Here, chosen more or less at random, are some typical extracts from the diaries of these years:

Monday 30th January 1882:
Holiday today and town gaily decorated for opening of George A. Clark Town Hall. In morning went down to office to get letter – also at Express office. Home for an hour studying. Then went with Bella, Jessie and John to office and saw procession pass from 12.30 to 1.30. Saw father and Mr Crouch [his minister] on leaving office and went up with them to Semple's house and saw procession pass again. Home again for 45 minutes – Mrs Ross in – then at Mr Crouch's to dinner. Came home about 6 for an hour. Then called on Mr Gardiner about festival. Afterwards went out with family, Aunt Wilson and Bessie, and Aunt and Allan Leitch through town to see illuminations, fireworks from High Church and electric light at Town Hall where conversazione was being held.

Friday 3rd February 1882:
Called in morning at Liberal Club ... called on Rev. Dr Flett about obtaining Rev. W. H. Wylie as speaker at SS [Sabbath School] Union Service. Went down to Town Hall for Cantata

of Lady of the Lake. Chorus, orchestra and balcony in full dress – effect very fine. Cantata very well rendered.

Friday 7th April 1882:
Saw Mr Crouch in evening on leaving office. Went with Ellen tonight to Sacred Cantata of Esther rendered by Wallneuk Mission Choir and soloists in Good Templar Hall. Connective readings by Rev. Mr McLay of Free Middle Church who leaves shortly for new parish church, Rothesay. Attendance good and singing very enjoyable.

Tuesday 21st November 1882:
. . . After tea went down with Bella and Jane to train for Johnstone. Then went with John to School of Art where he joined the Chemistry Class. Afterwards at Liberal Club for a short time. Then at meeting of Parliamentary Debating Association where opposed Second Reading of Church & Manse Assessment Bill . . .

Saturday 14th January 1888:
Rose at 6. Wrote at essay till 8. Then had breakfast and worship and left for office at 9. Bella called at quarter to two to get text books to send to Ellen at Rothesay. Went to McNicols for lunch at 2. Back at office till 5 when home for tea. John in. After that John left and I wrote at essay till after 12. Went to bed at 1.

Monday 2nd April 1888:
Rose at quarter to seven. Took cold bath. Studied for some time. At office at quarter past nine. Had dinner in Royal Oak at quarter past one. At office till quarter past six, then at Liberal Club for half an hour and home. Two Misses Blackwood from Glasgow had been out in afternoon from Glasgow. After tea George and Mrs Cuthbertson called and waited till 9 o'clock. Studied till half past eleven when went to bed.

Monday 11th June 1888:

Rose at quarter to eight. Morning beautiful. Got 9.03 train to Glasgow. Met Mr Crouch at Paisley Station. Had dinner in Royal Oak at 2. Home at 7. Got Mary Nisbet to take Annie's place at Mossvale Penny Savings Bank. Then had tea and studied mechanics till shortly after 10.

Friday 22nd March 1889:

Rose about 7. At Sheriff Court Library from 9 to 10. Annie called at office after meeting of Christian Abstinence Association at 1. Had lunch at office at 2. Home at 5 for tea. Back at office at quarter past six. Annie called at quarter to seven. Went with her and James to Town Hall where great crowds to hear Grammar School concert. Very enjoyable. Over at 10. At office for some papers. To bed at quarter to eleven.

Thursday 2nd May 1889:

Rose at quarter to eight. At office about half past nine. Home for dinner at 1 and back at office at twenty minutes to two. Had tea in office at six. Remained at office till five minutes to eight when went to the Platform of Good Templar Hall where Lecture – most interesting and telling – delivered by Henry George on the Single Tax Proposal on land values alone. Resolution moved by Peter Eadie and seconded by J.M. McCallum. I moved Vote of Thanks to lecturer. Back at the office for a few minutes. Home at half past ten. To bed at half past eleven.

Friday 14th June 1889:

Rose at twenty minutes to eight. At office at half past nine. Home for dinner shortly before one and back at office shortly before two. Had refreshments at McNicols at half past five. Left office at eight and went home. Read Baedecker's Northern Germany till 10. To bed at quarter to eleven.

Friday 4th October 1889:

Rose at half past seven. At office until half past nine. Went to Glasgow by 9.48 train. Met Annie at Walker's. Saw Seal Jackets there. Also at Russ's. Then made business call. Had lunch at Smiths. Home by 3 o'clock train. Went at quarter to five to dinner of Incorporation of Merchants & Traders of Paisley. Very pleasant evening. Sang 'The Meeting of the Waters'. Replied to toast as a new member. Over shortly after 10 . . . home shortly after 11. To bed at 12.30.

Thursday 12th December 1889:

[After rising at half past five and a sponge bath] read St Martin's Eve. At Sheriff Clerk's about 9 and at office at half past nine. Home for dinner at half past one. Back at office about half past three. Went to Glasgow by train at half past five. Called at Russ's. Had tea in restaurant. Then at Shorthand Class. Went to Mitchell Library for a short time. Then at Elocution Class. Home by 9.20 train. At office till quarter past ten. Wrote to James. To bed at half past eleven.

These were all weekdays, or Saturdays which appear to have differed little from the rest of the week. Sundays were even busier than weekdays and the space for these days is fully filled in in his meticulous hand. One example is fairly typical:

November 3rd 1889:

Rose at quarter past eight. Weather very wet. At Barr Street at quarter past eleven. Gave address on 'The Path of the Just'. At church hall for lunch. Then in Deacon's Room. At committee meeting in reference to Band of Hope. In afternoon Annie at Mossvale Church. Good attendance at Victoria Place notwithstanding wet weather. Sermon by Mr Crouch. Thomas Paterson received in as member. Home for dinner. Back at class. 9 present. At teacher's meeting. Called at Alex Lang's. Then at Miss Connell's. Home at half past eight. Read and studied. Had hot bath. To bed at eleven.

At the time of the 1891 census Tom and Annie were living at 103 Greenock Road. The house is recorded in the roll as having five rooms with one or more windows. What is surprising to us today is that in this relatively small and still childless establishment there is a maidservant, Jeannie Alexander.

In 1891 Tom bought the house in which he and Annie were to live for the rest of their lives, Hazelwood, Castlehead, at a price of £950 (about £100,000 in present-day money, quite a substantial purchase for a young solicitor). He had a mortgage from the First Paisley 158th Economic Building Society of £1000, or more than 100% of the purchase price, which suggests he had a good relationship with the First Paisley 158th Economic Building Society. On 19 May in the same year he transferred the title of the house to Annie, a prudent step then as now for a solicitor practising without the benefit of limited liability. The generous loan from the First Paisley 158th Economic Building Society was not needed for long, and was repaid in October 1906. In 1910 he took out a fresh mortgage of £500 with the Renfrewshire District Branch of British Order of Ancient Free Gardeners Friendly Society, possibly as a response to the default of the building clients, which could well have taken place at this time as a result of the 1909 Budget.

Castlehead, then as now, is a slightly anomalous little enclave, a quintessentially leafy Victorian suburb right in the middle of downtown Paisley. It is built on a gentle hill (another candidate for Vanduara) and is composed of three roads known unimaginatively as High Road, Low Road and Main Road. The houses on the three roads are substantial villas, all but one built around the middle of Victoria's reign. The remaining house is an old house and with the gift for imaginative naming which seems to be a feature of Castlehead is known as 'The Auld House'. At the beginning of the twentieth century the villas were inhabited by substantial bourgeoisie, and to live there would be a mark of having arrived. It was, as estate agents might have said, very conveniently situated for access to the town centre. Tom was able to walk to his office, which, although moving from time to time, was always near Paisley Cross, about a mile away, and as he made his way there he would see the daily progress in the demolition of the single-storey thatched cottages and their replacement with yellow and red sandstone blocks of flats which must have looked like extravagantly decorated skyscrapers.

The generous local provision of railway stations meant that there was a choice available, but West Station, which will make a melancholy appearance later in this narrative, was the closest, being just perhaps five minutes away, the railway line leading to it passing immediately below Hazelwood.

Hazelwood was and is a good-sized villa. In those days it had a large garden (part of which is now occupied by another house). My main recollection of the garden is of huge rhododendron bushes. I cannot remember ever seeing them in flower, and indeed until I was in my 20s I do not know that I was aware that rhododendrons were not always dark green and sombre, but on the contrary could be colourful to the point of vulgarity. What I do remember is that the trains which passed along the railway line at the bottom of the garden deposited soot on the leaves of the rhododendrons (perhaps inhibiting their flowering) so that we all got rather dirty when my balsawood model aeroplane landed on top of one of the bushes and my Uncle Douglas had to retrieve it with a walking stick.

The path from the road to the front door was one which Annie recalled that Tom sometimes walked up whistling. When this happened she knew that a rich client had died and there was a substantial executry estate to be wound up. I never knew Tom, whistling or otherwise, but I do remember the front door to which the path led. It was partly composed of sand-blasted glass, and the handle was of amber-coloured glass. Annie, or to me 'Granny', was always a kind and welcoming figure: 'Come away in, come away in'. I liked her – and not only because of her sensible views on the preferability of little boys to little girls ('nobler') or of the fact that she gave me a silver sixpence for repeating The Lord's Prayer. In the front of the house, to the right, was a dining room with a large round table which I had fun extending by cranking a little handle. Behind it was the Parlour, where the tiddlywinks were kept in a brown wooden cup. On the wall was a print of a Victorian allegorical painting, I think *The Man with the Muckrake*. I suspect other allegorical paintings hung elsewhere in the house.

Upstairs and to the front was a large drawing room with an electric radiogram on which, having put in a new steel needle, we could play what were not then called 78s: Harry Lauder, Gigli, Amelita Galli-Curci, *Only a Rose, Rio Rita, The Trumpeter*, hymns and sacred music.

I know little about the family's holidays after Tom and Annie's early backpacking except that there was an annual holiday at Millport on the Isle of Cumbrae for a month every Easter. The family took a house there and Ronald told me that behind it was a bank which was thick with primroses. I recall this because it is one of only two occasions when I can remember Ronald showing any interest in flowers or even a knowledge of their names. Tom and Annie took a maid with them each year, but on one occasion she did not return with them, having, sadly, died at Millport.

The electric radiogram on the face of it seems rather inappropriate in what was essentially a Victorian home, but Tom and Annie had a positive zest for embracing modernity. In addition to Tom's dictating machine at his office, the house had an electric washing machine and an electrical machine for peeling potatoes, and various other labour-saving devices – all the more surprising at a time when labour was cheap and readily available.

This was the home in which Ernest and his brothers were brought up. It was a comfortable home and a loving home. The standard of living was high, but it was achieved by very hard work on Tom's part, and the boys were not spoiled or encouraged to take their good fortune for granted. As well as the immediate family, Ernest and his brothers were surrounded by a more extended, but very close, family who took much interest in each other and spent a lot of time visiting each other. The church, liberalism and temperance were real influences. The forces for material and moral progress had achieved much, but there was no assumption that there was not still more to be done.

Tom as he emerges from the factual evidence of his diaries is a powerful character, and, whether genetically or by example, Ernest cannot fail to have been influenced by him. Tom's application and seriousness would be surprising at any age; for a young man in his mid-twenties his self-discipline is astonishing. His professional life is to be advanced by studying elocution and shorthand. He is considering taking a correspondence university degree (a sort of Open University). He is acquiring knowledge for its own sake: Latin, Greek, physics. He is civically active: he joins in founding the Parliamentary Debating Association, he espouses Esperanto, he supports proportional representation and Liberal politics. There is fun, such as Hallowe'en parties, and family life. Above all there is the Church and all its various activities, religious and moral. To describe it as a full life is to understate his purposeful existence. Tom was not physically robust, but he was possessed of a dynamic energy focused certainly on the advancement of his career and his family's prosperity, but even more on the cause of moral and spiritual progress.

4

The Growing Boy

THE INFLUENCES OF YOUTH

Annie was much troubled by miscarriages and her three sons arrived at roughly five-yearly intervals: Douglas in 1893, Ernest in 1897, and Ronald in 1903. Indeed Ronald was only born after a régime of nine months' bed rest which would not be prescribed by a modern gynaecologist. 'Ronald' was a family name, but 'Douglas' and 'Ernest' do not appear to have been. Why they were chosen I do not know, but it is not difficult to imagine that 'Ernest' appealed because of the qualities suggested by its adjectival homonym. Tom and Annie would not know that in raffish London circles in the 1890s, 'earnest', like 'musical', was a code word for homosexual, so that there were knowing smiles on the opening night of Oscar Wilde's most popular play. Ernest was not earnest in either sense, but earnestness was a quality that his father would have regarded as eminently desirable.

His name was registered at birth as 'Ernest Thomas Reid', and it was always as 'Ernest' that he was known, but in every record and document other than his birth certificate, his name is given as 'Thomas Ernest Reid'.

Douglas's secondary education was at Glasgow High School, while Ernest and Ronald, like Hugh McPherson, went to Paisley Grammar School. Why there was this distinction, I know not: it may have had something to do with the defaulting clients, or it may simply have been a decision that flowed from where Tom was spending the bulk of his time at different dates. Glasgow High School was founded as the Grammar School of Glasgow in the twelfth century, but its roots go back to the foundation of the Cathedral. It is proud of its distinguished list of old boys, which includes Colin Campbell, who commanded the Highland Brigade in the Crimea, and Bonar Law, who was the leader of the Conservative Party throughout the First World War, and briefly Prime Minister after it. Paisley Grammar School was instituted by a Royal Charter signed in 1576 by a precocious King James VI of Scotland, aged ten: one of the witnesses was his tutor, George Buchanan, scholar, historian and poet, known throughout Europe as a man of the Rennaissance. The School is certainly older, its origins going back to the early days of Paisley Abbey. Like Glasgow High School, it is a shining example of the tradition that made Scottish schooling a by-word throughout the world, providing rigorous education to uncompromising standards for pupils of ability, whatever their financial background.

Initially there were two teachers at Paisley Grammar School for the town's 800 inhabitants. The head teacher, or Master, taught the higher branches of education, essentially Latin, and his assistant, the Doctor, taught English, writing and arithmetic, as well as running the Sang Scuil. The school's serious purpose is grimly reflected in its wonderfully uncompromising motto: *Disce Puer Aut Abi*: 'Learn, Child, or Begone'! The quality of the education is reflected in the fact that by the nineteenth century Professors of Glasgow University examined the Latin and Greek classes. Until well into that century, the classics were indeed the dominant part of the curriculum. In 1836 the Professors commended the Rector for not deviating into 'departments of study quite foreign to classical literature, and unsuitable for boys at the age best fitted to acquiring its elements . . . mathematics and the modern languages . . . Now, mathematics is above the comprehension of and repugnant to the feeling of boys at the age alluded to, and as for modern languages, they are easily and best acquired by young men after they have finished their studies – the classics – which form the best foundation upon which to rear all mental superstructures, whether literary or scientific'. In the 1860s the limited scope of the curriculum was addressed. A new building in Gothic style was to complement the existing one. The change in the philosophy of the school was reflected by a change, fortunately only temporary, in its name, to Paisley Grammar School and Academy, as Mathematics, Algebra, Book-keeping, French, German and Italian were added to the traditional diet of English, Arithmetic, Latin and Greek. In 1885 a laboratory was built.

It is difficult to make a comparison between the Scottish standards of secondary and tertiary education and those of other countries in the nineteenth century, but the disproportionately high numbers of Scots of the diaspora eminent in the professions in England and throughout the Empire attest to some superiority, even allowing for the effect of emigration from the Highlands and other areas. As is well known, John Knox had referred to the duty of providing education for all children, and the Education Acts of the Scottish Parliament of 1684 and 1696 required that a school be established in every parish. By the mid-nineteenth century the proportions of children receiving secondary education were:

Scotland – 1 out of 205 school pupils
Prussia – 1 out of 249
France – 1 out of 570
England – 1 out of 1,300

The ratio of university pupils to population in Scotland was twice that of Prussia, and six times that of England.

Paisley Grammar School had been situated for centuries on the Oakshaw ridge. Hugh McPherson was taught there in the third Grammar School, a pleasant Regency box, and in the Gothic Grammar School and Academy of 1863. But in 1898 there was a move from the old school buildings, in cramped accommodation, unevenly built and with very small playgrounds attached to them, to a modern building, recognisably a school, in the more open ground to the east of the town centre. Ernest was one of the first generation of pupils in what is the present school.

The cost of the education at Paisley Grammar School was heavily subsidised by endowments and by the town council, and was waived altogether for those who could not afford it. *The History of Paisley Grammar School,* published in 1875, gives details of the fees in force in the early 1870s. The fee per quarter in each of the Divisions of the school (Latin, Greek, Latin and Greek, French, German) was 10s.6d. ('No charge to be made against any Pupil attending Arithmetic only'). 'To prevent desultory attendance, Pupils (with certain exceptions) returning after any Quarter Day are charged the full fee for that Quarterly Term, as in many cases such Pupils give more trouble than those who joined at the proper time.' Even allowing for inflation, these fees (currently equivalent to about £200 per annum per Department) were not high. All the same, and despite the presence of some for whom fees would be waived, the atmosphere of the school was distinctly middle class, though not socially élitist to any great extent. Hugh McPherson, describing the school some 25 years before Ernest went there, recalled that:

> The pupils of the school were the sons and daughters of middle-class families of Paisley and the surrounding country-side – merchants, industrialists, ministers, doctors, lawyers, the landed gentry and farmers. Only a few of the wealthiest families sent their sons to English public schools or to their exotic counterparts in Scotland. The Grammar School was the gateway to the university, for it was one of those west country reservoirs from which Glasgow University drew the bulk of its students.

Like all such Scottish schools, the classes were mixed, the boys and girls sitting in two parallel rows of benches.

After winning his prizes, scholastic and athletic, Ernest went on to Glasgow University to study law in the session 1914/15. He went as the holder of the Macfarlane Bursary. This Bursary was one of three established in memory of a Paisley solicitor, given by preference to young men connected with Paisley. They were worth £33 a year each. Ernest's was awarded for three years and was determined by performance in the General Bursary

Competition in Arts, a competition in which there was a great deal of interest from schools throughout Scotland in the days before university grants.

Glasgow University is a pre-Reformation foundation, the second oldest university in Scotland. The Scottish universities had relatively little connection with the ancient universities in England, Oxford and Cambridge, as membership of these universities, until the nineteenth century, was available only to those who acknowledged the religious supremacy of the Crown. The Scottish universities looked rather to Europe, and had a close connection with the continental universities, with which they still share certain traditions. Until late in the nineteenth century, there were only two universities in England, whereas Scotland, with its much smaller population, had four. Their rôle in Scottish education and in the formation of Scottish national culture was crucial, but at least until the reforms effected by the Scottish Universities Commission between 1889 and 1897, the Scottish universities were not directly comparable with Oxford and Cambridge. By the 1880s there had been many complaints about the inferiority of Scottish university teaching. Scottish students were described as 'the handloom weavers of the intellectual world'. The failure rate was high. In the Glasgow University Junior Latin Class in 1889–1890, 200 candidates failed out of 255. The Younger Pitt famously went to Cambridge at the age of 14. But he was unusually precocious and he went at a time when, according to Gibbon, Oxford (and presumably Cambridge) was very lax and undemanding. In Scotland, on the other hand, as late as 1878 students were still regularly going to University at the same age. Those who went on to Oxford and Cambridge appear to have gone in at the same level as English schoolboys. Hugh McPherson describes himself as doing in his Latin and Greek classes at Glasgow 'the same kind of work as was done in the higher forms of English public schools, from which lads went to Oxford and Cambridge about the age of 18. We Scottish students nearly all started our college life about 16 years of age. The Latin and Greek classes at Glasgow were huge classes of two or three hundred students'. Despite the reforms, there was not the stimulation of one-to-one tutorials: the teaching was severely didactic and students were expected simply to learn what was taught to them. This would be particularly true in the Law Faculty in Ernest's time. Because of the cost of producing textbooks for the small market of Scottish lawyers, there were few textbooks, succeeding editions of Bell's *Principles* (which had been first published as far back as 1829) being about all that was available, as Ronald was to recall. Then, and indeed still in the 1960s, the printing press might as well not have been invented: lecturers read, or dictated, and students slavishly copied down, to learn by rote. Then, though not in the 1960s, argument, discussion or dissent would not be expected or welcomed.

Ernest travelled by train from Paisley. It was a tough régime: Hugh McPherson described 'getting up about 6 a.m. and catching a train about 7 a.m. (after a walk of over a mile), then a two mile walk from Central Station to Gilmorehill, where classes opened at 8 a.m.'

Ernest had no difficulties with the work in the only session he completed before going to the War. He passed the Arts Preliminary Examination in Latin at the Higher standard and already came from school with passes in the Leaving Certificate at Higher standard in Mathematics and passes in English and French which appear only to have had one standard. In the session which ended in March 1915 he passed in Forensic Medicine with 70% and in Civil Law (Roman Law) with 84%. Had he continued, he would have had classes in Jurisprudence, Public International Law, Law of Scotland, Constitutional Law and History, Conveyancing, Political Economy, Mercantile Law, International Private Law and Evidence and Procedure. In the session 1915/16 he must have embarked on some of these classes, but he did not sit the examinations. By then he had gone to the War

War broke out on 4 August 1914. The reaction is well known. All over Europe there was a rush to join the colours. In Berlin they shouted 'To Paris'; in Paris 'To Berlin'. In London the response to

Kitchener's appeal for volunteers was such that *The Times* reported that 'mounted police were necessary to hold them [the volunteers] in check and the gates were only opened to admit six at a time'. Scotland's contribution was disproportionately high. Scotland had always contributed more than her share to Britain's armies. This was not simply for economic reasons: in 1914, there was no new economic stimulus, but there was a greater response to the call to arms in Scotland than anywhere else in Britain. In Glasgow the Corporation voted to equip two battalions from the tramway employees. Within the day one in six had volunteered – over 1,000 men – and by the end of the year 1,756 men had enlisted. The patriotic response was sufficient to split the ranks of both the women's movement and the Labour Party. Within the year over a quarter of Scotland's coalminers had enlisted and the government had to ban further enlistment in order to preserve the industry. Glasgow supplied enough able-bodied men to form 26 battalions. Twenty-four out of every 1,000 in the city joined up, a higher proportion than in any other British city. The University and Technical College together with the Chamber of Commerce between them supplied the whole of the 17th Battalion of the Highland Light Infantry. In total 26 battalions of the Highland Light Infantry were raised during the War and 11,000 officers and men were killed in action. Throughout the War the silent cinema screens proclaimed the words:

> Where Scotland's thistle sways on High,
> And foemen meet here knee to knee,
> Blow up the pipes and then ye'll see
> Her courage wake,
> And learn how Scotland's sons can die for
> Empire's sake.

Scotland's population was a tenth of England's, but Scottish regiments made up a seventh of the whole British Army.

A Scottish officer writing of the scenes in regimental depots in August 1914 said:

During this period we had great difficulties to contend with. We had to house and feed all recruits; they came in so fast that it was impossible for us to deal with them and despatch them to their units on the same day. It sometimes happened too that, although we had practically cleared the barracks one evening, there would be some 400 recruits on parade the following morning, those having come in during the night.

Another officer wrote:

The glamour of the kilt was irresistible. In Glasgow and the west of Scotland hundreds flocked to enlist in the famous regiment [the Cameronians]. The Glasgow Stock Exchange had, in an incredibly short time raised a special company of its own, and not to be outdone, the students of the university followed suit. Then for a few days every north-bound train carried its complement of recruits to the Cameron Depot. Soon the barracks were crowded out.

A. J. C. Moir wrote:

My brother was lost at Loos: he was reported missing and no further information was ever received although we learnt he had survived the first terrible day, and was lost early next morning when some advanced posts were given up.

My brother was a student at Glasgow Technical College, and 'joined up' when the appeal was made in September or October 1914. His platoon was composed entirely of University or Technical College students – privates all. Alas, few of them were ever to see Scotland again.

Few people now understand the high motives and disregard for self interest that activated these young lads at that terrible time.

What was the reason for this incredible reaction? The answer is a complex one and not easy for us to understand. There was certainly a degree of simple jingoism, such as prompted Ronald to inscribe 'Smash the Kaiser' in the fly-leaf of one of his books; although most accounts of the atmosphere in Britain on 4 August 1914 stress the solemn response to the call. And few people knew what war was like. In Britain, as opposed to continental Europe, there was little xenophobia (which is different from, and even less attractive than, jingoism). What there was, was a feeling that had built up over the previous 15 or 20 years, as crises succeeded each other in the Balkans and elsewhere, and as Germany's naval ambitions were noted, a feeling that a confrontation with an aggressive Germany could not be put off much longer. German (more often called Prussian) militarism was seen as the very simple explanation for the events of 1914, particularly the attack on Belgium; and there was a quiet recognition that this militarism had to be checked if a pacific existence were to continue. This view was well expressed by Sir Edward Grey, in his speech in the House of Commons on 4 August 1914, when, echoing Gladstone, he said that Britain could not stand by and watch 'the unchecked aggrandisement' of any one continental power. His speech had a crucial influence on those Liberals and Radicals who were hesitant about seeing Britain enter the war.

But allied to this was that concept of duty which we find difficult today to understand. Throughout the nineteenth century, praised by the poets and sustained by examples of heroism and steadfastness by Britain's imperial soldiers and intrepid explorers, an ideal had been created that could be traced to classical times and that was reinforced by the strength of Christian belief. Episodes like the end of Scott's expedition to the Antarctic not only illustrated a standard of behaviour, but in a very real degree by their cumulative effect encouraged it. The schoolbooks of the time were full of accounts of behaviour to be admired and heroes (and heroines like Grace Darling and Florence Nightingale) to be emulated. For boys in particular there was a literature of derring-do in books such as Henty's, and magazines like *The Boy's Own Paper* ('The *B.O.P.*'). The Boy Scouts' Association (of which Ronald, certainly, and Ernest, probably, were enthusiastic members) crystallised these Victorian values and impressed them on a wide membership.

The founder of that movement, Baden-Powell, merits some study as a soldier (a Lieutenant-General, although not well regarded by his superiors in South Africa), a spokesman for the Establishment, and above all an unparalleled influence on the youth of the day, after the publication in 1908 of *Scouting for Boys*.

Baden-Powell (pronounced, he said, as in 'Bathing-Towel') sought to mould young men in a way that he felt was good for them; what he prescribed was also a model for the formation of dutiful servants of the imperial ideal. Sports, manliness, self-discipline and duty to the state were the qualities to be fostered; what was to be eradicated was loafing, hooliganism, watching football and listening to agitators.

Here he is on football spectators:

Thousands of boys or young men, pale, narrow-chested, hunched up, miserable specimens, smoking endless cigarettes, numbers of them betting, all of them learning to be hysterical as they groan and cheer in panic unison with their neighbours – the worst sound of all being the hysterical scream of laughter that greets any little trip or fall of a player.

What was to be aimed for was the promotion of self-control, the concealment of feelings. The objective was 'manhood, unmoved by panic or excitement, and reliable in the tightest of places. Get the lads ready for this – teach them to be manly, to play the game . . . and not be merely onlookers and loafers'.

Some of this is incontestably good sense, aiming at ensuring that young men perhaps from deprived backgrounds live their lives to the full, and make the most of their capacities; but there does seem also to be an element of formation of ideal citizens for an idealised state, a sort of social engineering that co-existed with the Social Darwinism of the time.

It was a time when being English was described as 'having drawn the winning ticket in the lottery of life', and it is easy to see

Baden-Powell as aiming for the promotion of a world master-race. But that is unfair, and Scouts were to fight bravely against Fascism, which was the antithesis of the régime of fair play that B.-P. had admired; but he certainly did think, as most of his contemporaries did, that England (and it would be of England rather than of Britain that they thought) was, without argument, superior in all its qualities to any other country in the world, and that in that world the British Empire was a force for good and progress for which its citizens should be prepared without hesitation to fight and lay down their lives.

Scouts, and Cub Scouts and Rover Scouts, and King's Scouts (of whom Ronald was one) and Scoutmasters poured into the movement, presided over by Baden-Powell, with his modest title, Chief Scout of the World; and girls flocked into their own hierarchy of Guides, at the top of which, keeping it in the family, was Lady Baden-Powell. In *Great Contemporaries,* Churchill provided an appreciation of the movement:

In 1908 the Chief Scout, as he called himself, published his book, *Scouting for Boys*. It appealed to all the sense of adventure and love of open-air life which is so strong in youth. But beyond this it stirred those sentiments of knightly chivalry, of playing the game – any game – earnest or fun – hard and fairly, which constitute the most important part of the British system of education.

The Chief Scout's prose is so marvellously of its time, so ripe for satire and so unconsciously self-parodying, that it is tempting to quote it at great length, but here are just three excerpts from *Aids to Scoutsmastership* to point up his intentions and suggest their relevance to service of the state:

A nation to be prosperous must be well disciplined, and you only get discipline in the mass by discipline in the individual. By discipline I mean obedience to authority and to other dictates of duty. The first Law, namely, A Scout's honour is to be trusted (A Scout is Trustworthy), is one on which the whole of the Scout's future behaviour and discipline hangs. The Scout is expected to be straight.

[The Scout] should have that confidence in himself which will give him the hope and pluck in time of stress in the struggle of life, which will encourage him to stick it out till he achieves success.

Loyalty to country is of the highest value for keeping men's views balanced and in the proper perspective. The external signs, such as saluting the flag, standing for the National Anthem, and so on, help in promoting this, but the essential thing is the development of the true spirit which underlies such demonstrations.

Those who were most inspired and instructed by this culture were the young men of Ernest's age and class. They were steeped in the traditions and the literature of the time. Poems that praised courage, heroism and the manly virtues were not embarrassing or bizarre to them. Indeed the popular books of poetry at the time were full of such works. In 1919, Keynes looked at the new House of Commons and said that it seemed to be full of hard-faced men who looked as if they had done well out of the war. In *Put out More Flags*, Evelyn Waugh's Basil Seal, who was a cynical Bright Young Thing, a creature of the brittle Twenties, reacted to the arrival of the Second World War by saying that he wanted to be one of the hard-faced men who did well out of it. But Basil's contemporaries had seen the Somme and Third Ypres/Passchendaele; Ernest's contemporaries had not. And of course Basil's cultural traditions were too strong, and in the event he went into the Commandos to be a hero.

The sort of men who became the subalterns of 1914–18 have been described as belonging to a club, which shared the same code and the same values and could be relied on to behave in the same ways. Dr Arnold's teachings at Rugby had permeated the whole of the élite education system, not only the Public Schools. Expressions like 'playing the game' and 'doing the decent thing' and all the attitudes of the clubland of John Buchan or Sapper or Dornford Yates that we find amusing or incredible were received as givens in these years and formed part of a common culture of the middle and upper classes. It is easy to see the cultural assumptions of the time as a conscious exercise in brainwashing designed to create an officer corps, a class to govern the Empire. That it was not in fact any part of a deliberate campaign, and that the culture developed spontaneously, does not make it any the less powerful. Ernest and his contemporaries were programmed for duty, and many of them for death.

It is instructive that whereas Tom Brown was the hero for Ernest and his contemporaries, for us it is Flashman. An absence of irony, cynicism and iconoclasm distinguishes Ernest's genera-tion from ours. Oscar Wilde, Shaw, H. H. Munro, Lytton Strachey and others were certainly active, but their influence was confined to a small section of society. In as far as they were known outside that section, they were regarded with suspicion and distaste. For the bulk of society, whether working, middle or upper class, 'bolshevites', socialists, republicans and other minorities that threatened the *status quo* were dangerous and immoral. Society was infinitely more deferential and hierarchical than it is now, and to question the way it was ordered was to put oneself beyond the pale of decency. Those in authority were entitled – simply by virtue of their office – to immunity from criticism, and the more elevated their office, the more it became irreligious to question their worth. Great men were there to be respected. When Strachey and others suggested that they were human, their biographies were characterised with contempt as 'debunking' – though by present standards the criticism they contained was very modest.

In this context the concept of unthinking duty was unchal-lenged, and it was reinforced by the very strong religious beliefs of these years, by the institutions of army and empire and by the educational prominence of the classical world of Greece and Rome: views on the duty of service to the state struck a chord that echoed from the Roman Empire to the Victorian Empire.

The sentimental ballads that were sung at that time, glorifying death on distant frontiers of the Empire and the sacrifice of selfish happiness to duty, were not sung in a spirit of self-mockery, and the anthologies did not contain as quaint curiosities poems like Tennyson's superb patriotic narrative *The Revenge,* or *Vitaï Lampada* by the great celebrator of Victorian virtues, Sir Henry Newbolt:

> There's a breathless hush in the Close to-night
>   Ten to make and the match to win
> A bumping pitch and a blinding light,
>   An hour to play and the last man in.
> And it's not for the sake of a ribboned coat,
>   Or the selfish hope of a season's game,
> But his Captain's hand on his shoulder smote
>   'Play up! play up! and play the game!'
>
> The sand of the desert is sodden red,
>   Red with the wreck of a square that broke;
> The Gatling's jammed and the colonel dead;
>   And the regiment blind with dust and smoke.
> The river of death has brimmed his banks,
>   And England's far, and Honour a name,
> But the voice of a schoolboy rallies the ranks,
>   'Play up! play up! and play the game!'

War is a noble game. The poem was written in 1897. Newbolt came to dislike it. 'It's a kind of Frankenstein's Monster that I created thirty years ago,' he complained in 1923. But it was well received both by the critics and by the general public at the time, and, significantly, it enjoyed a revival of popularity with the outbreak of the First World War. Interestingly, when the war broke out, Newbolt was recruited to the War Propaganda Bureau to help to shape public opinion.

One of the casualties of the Great War was the belief in Progress, a belief which was born in the Age of Reason, animated by Faith and sustained and strengthened through the nineteenth century by the development of science and industry, by utilitarian philosophy, by the spread of education, by the process, exemplified in the great Parliamentary Commissions, of gathering evidence, analysing it and refining a strategy of action. It was not only a British phenomenon. Indeed a feature of those years was the international freemasonry open to those of comfortable means and good education, who enjoyed the privilege of easy physical travel (Britons required no passport in 1914 though they sometimes found it convenient to carry one) and of an equal spiritual access to like-minded advanced communities throughout Western Europe and the New World. Henry James and E. M. Forster are examples of the type. And Haldane's studies of philosophy and literature at Heidelberg illustrate the integrity of pre-War Europe; just as his enforced resignation because he had referred to the Germany of his studies as his 'spiritual home' illustrates the end of this easy internationalism.

There were of course dissenters, some who, as a result of economic theory or an interpretation of evolutionary ideas, regarded the future with pessimism. But as the twentieth century began, the huge majority of educated, serious men and women believed that despite setbacks, and not without effort, the graph of human material wellbeing and indeed happiness would continue to move upwards.

By 1918 this belief no longer existed. Some individuals bravely continued to look to the future with optimism. Smuts declared at the end of the war that the great march of civilisation was under way again. But the near-unanimous assumption of inexorable progress had submerged in the mud of Flanders and it has never been extricated. A degree of idealism was invested in the establishment of the League of Nations, but its machinations were not impressive and, at its birth, the translation of President Wilson's lofty Fourteen Points into crude horse-trading at the Peace Conferences revealed the moral vacuum which the war had left. The United Nations Organisation, which replaced the League after the Second World

War, never really attempted to enshrine an ideal. If it has in fact been more effective than the League, that is perhaps because it recognised reality. The nearest thing to an institutionalised ideal since 1918 may be the European Union, which owed its foundation to men who had lived through the two Wars and who took steps so to arrange access to Europe's resources that there would be an end to the series of civil wars that had ravaged the continent for a thousand years and that twice tore it asunder in the twentieth century.

The attitudes with which men went to war in 1914 and 1939 were profoundly different. In 1939 men were prepared to fight because there was clearly no alternative. Conscription and not volunteering was the route to the barracks. Some went to lengths to avoid fighting, but for the most part it was recognised that there was an enemy that had at last to be confronted. There was none of the heady enthusiasm, the ecstasy of volunteering of 1914. There was not the spirit of a crusade.

And that was despite the fact that in reality 1939 *was* a crusade and 1914 was not. The lines between good and the vilest of evils were drawn with a clarity that is rare in human conflict: for humanity and not just for Britain, Nazism had indeed to be destroyed if the world were not as Churchill famously put it 'to fall into a new Dark Age made more sinister, and perhaps more protracted, by the lights of perverted science'. To quote Professor John Lukacs, writing of Churchill, 'It was good to know that summer [of 1940] . . . that the struggle was ineluctable; that . . . there were still two camps as close to Good Versus Evil as ever in the terrestrial struggles of nations'. It was in this sense that A. J. P. Taylor described the Second World War as 'a good war'.

Things were far from so clear-cut in 1914, certainly so far as Britain was concerned. Germany was a modern, civilised democracy. It was not demonstrably evil and it did not directly threaten British security. The technical *casus belli*, the attack on Belgium, was found in a long-forgotten treaty obligation of the sort that *realpolitik* regularly overlooks, and the decision to go to war (which was achieved only at the cost of Cabinet resignations) was based on the nice calculation, even today challenged for example by Professor Niall Ferguson, that it was not in Britain's interests to see the continent dominated by Germany. As late as 29 July 1914, just six days before Britain entered the war, the King was informed by Asquith that British involvement in the conflict was unlikely.

But the delicacy of the political decision was not reflected in the popular enthusiasm for the war. Rupert Brooke's poetry is often quoted as illustrative of the mood in 1914. Another typical voice is that of Asquith's son, Herbert (or 'Beb'), who addressed Ares, the Greek God of War:

> Death is nothing, life an empty name;
> Arise and lead us 'ere our blood be tame,
> Lord of Thunder, Ares of the Crimson Mail!

Brooke died on his way to fight and he remains in history as the happy warrior. Beb's life was longer and sadder and an eloquent explanation of the difference in the mood of 1939. He went to France and fought as an infantry officer in the early part of the war before the effects of prolonged exposure in the trenches were understood. Later, troops were withdrawn from the front line after a few days, but Beb and his men were not. When he came home on leave there was clearly something seriously wrong with him, but shell shock, or post-traumatic stress, was not yet known. He did not have a doctor like Rivers, who was to treat Sassoon and Owen, and even some of his family thought he was simply drinking too much. After great suffering he recovered to a degree, and bravely insisted on going back to France, where he served as a courageous and able artillery officer, frequently in a very dangerous forward observation rôle.

He survived, but he was broken by his experiences. He did not resume his career in law; he attempted to earn his living as a writer with only a little success. The effects of shell shock returned and he did now drink to excess: he had much to forget.

It is not difficult to see why, after the experiences that Beb and his contemporaries went through, their successors viewed war with a cool realism. What is more difficult is to understand why Beb and Brooke and all the others had hailed Ares of the Crimson Mail with such enthusiasm in the first place, why they jostled to enlist, why they bore the horrors and terrors of the Western Front and Gallipoli so stoically, why they fought and died and never complained. In another of his poems, *The Volunteer,* Beb expresses the mood of the time:

> Nor needs he any hearse to bear him hence,
> Who goes to join the men of Agincourt.

Even Churchill, emotional certainly, and romantic, but not so given to poetic fantasy, talked of 'the moral satisfaction of fighting for your country and the glory of dying in battle on its behalf'. How was it that Britain saw herself as fighting not for her own advantage, but in a titanic struggle, which manifestly was not taking place, against an evil that challenged all the values of civilisation and humanity?

Of course there are important lessons to be learned from the self-fulfilling influence of a series of crises and colonial rivalries that made war seem inevitable when it was far from being so. That, and the fact that there had not been a major conflict for 99 years, accounts for some of the euphoria of 1914. But it does not account for what is more remarkable: the quiet determination, once that early euphoria had subsided, with which those young men faced their destiny.

Beb and Churchill were entirely sincere, and their attitudes were far from unique. But even those who would not have agreed that Death was nothing and life an empty name (and Ernest would, I think, have been one) did not question the right of the country to demand their service in war. They acknowledged it to be their duty to submit without question to orders, and to execute them to the best of their ability, whatever might be the consequences. It is as well that such attitudes have long since disappeared, but we, in our individualist age, must try to understand them if we hope to enter into a condition of mind that may be separated from us by only two generations, but that is in a sense as remote as the code of the Samurai.

Ernest could not fail to be a son of the British Empire which, as was well known, covered one quarter of the earth when he was born. The Empire (sometimes known as the Second British Empire) that developed after the loss of the American colonies was not acquired altruistically. Commerce, strategical considerations and prestige were the motives that gave Britain her Empire, but the acquisition was rationalised and nobler justifications for Empire were discovered. To be fair, these nobler purposes were genuinely espoused by very many of those involved. Before the imperial episode was concluded it was evident that maintaining the Empire cost more than the benefits it brought to Britain, so the commercial or exploitative aspect of Empire in its later stages must be in doubt; what is not in doubt is the courage of explorers and collectors who sought to bring back knowledge of unknown continents, the devotion of missionaries who took Christianity and healing to the colonies, and the idealism of administrators who sought to provide good governance and to extirpate cruel and vicious customs.

Their actions and their assumptions must be judged by the standards of their time and not of ours, and the same must be said of the Laureate of Empire, Rudyard Kipling, whose stories and verse provided a crucial cultural background for men and women of Ernest's generation. Kipling was a complex man, many of whose views appear contradictory, and he has been to a degree unfairly caricatured for many years. He was not a narrow jingoist: he hated the excesses of Empire and despised the 'jelly-bellied flag-flappers'. He was much less of a racial supremacist than most of his contemporaries. He saw Britain's rôle in terms of responsibility rather than privilege. In his misunderstood *Recessional*, when he talks of the 'white man's burden', he is saying to Americans that they must now accept some of that responsibility. That may be patronising, but it is not exploitative or triumphalist.

It was an Imperial event, the Jameson Raid in 1895, that

prompted Kipling to write his most famous poem. *If* was phenomenally popular and Ernest would know it well. Its tone of silent stoicism was the expression of the current ideal, an ideal which would be attained

> If you can force your heart and nerve and sinew
>   To serve your turn long after they are gone,
> And so hold on when there is nothing in you
>   Except the Will which says to them: 'Hold On.'

Sir Hugh McPherson (as he had become) retired before India had gained her independence, but by then his son, Duncan, was working there as a railway engineer. When Duncan announced that he planned to leave on Independence, accompanied by his young bride, Joan, with an embryonic Janet in her womb, to make his career in Britain, Sir Hugh was displeased, because he felt it was Duncan's duty to stay and make Independence work for India.

When Janet (who had long since left Joan's womb) and I were in Stornoway on our honeymoon we watched a re-release of the old colonial adventure *Sanders of the River* in the local cinema. At the line, 'We British govern by love', even the Hebridean audience dissolved into hoots of laughter; but the line was not meant to be funny, and would have seemed commonplace when the film was first shown. Ideals, and the concept of ideals, were serious matters at the beginning of the twentieth century.

Ernest was too young to volunteer in August 1914. What he could, he did: he joined the University Officer Training Corps on 28 October 1914 as soon as he was eligible and duly became a cadet corporal. By 29 May 1915 he was old enough to enlist and he applied for a commission. (One of the questions on the application form was: 'Whether of pure European descent?'). On 11 June he was told that he was commissioned as a Second Lieutenant into the 3rd Battalion the Black Watch and was instructed to report to the Stirling School of Instruction on 15 June.

5

The Light of Common Day

THE BLACK WATCH

The influences that had formed Ernest till now had been essentially domestic: family and friends, church, school and university. But when he moved into the army, his character came to a final stage of formation, influenced not just by war and conflict, but by becoming in effect a member of a new family. General Sir Brian Horrocks, who was to command XXX Corps at Arnhem and was later a wonderfully relaxed and engaging television performer when he expounded with his sandbox the tactics of the Second World War battles, recalled that his company of the Middlesex Regiment had been attached to the Black Watch between the wars in Silesia. He remembered his time in the mess where he was even taught Highland dancing (easier in a kilt than a cavalryman's overalls): 'All regiments develop their own *esprit de corps* but it was impossible to live with the Black Watch and not realise that every officer and man whether Highlander or Lowlander belonged to one family, or rather to one clan'. As Horrocks said, every regiment has its own culture, but the Black Watch, because of its history and particular origin, had and has a particularly powerful sense of identity. One historian of the Regiment talked of 'the clan pride of the Black Watch [which] is still handed down as a sort of spiritual inheritance'. As early as 1822, its earliest historian recorded that 'in a Highland Regiment, every individual feels that his conduct is the subject of observation and that, independently of his duty, as one member of a systematic whole, he has a separate and individual reputation to sustain, which will be reflected on his family and district and glen'. The honour and traditions and prestige of the Regiment are keenly guarded and new members are under pressure to imbibe this culture and to strive to ensure that the ethos of the unit is preserved and passed on.

The modern distillation of that ethos is the professional confidence that prompts the Regiment to open its Home page with the words,

> We are the premier Scottish infantry Regiment in the British Army and one of the most famous fighting forces in the world. We combine the proud history and tradition of an organisation that has been soldiering for over 250 years with the skills and professionalism of a front-line unit in a modern Army.

It is difficult to identify the essence of the ethos. The soldiers of the Black Watch, 'the Watch', know that they are members of the best regiment in the British Army. If they are asked why they are the best, the circular reply is, 'Because we are the Black Watch'. If pressed, they will refer to the fierce reputation of the Regiment and its capacity for fighting its friends if there are no enemies to fight, and its tradition too of hospitality and friendship, the fact that 'everything you do you try to do well', the feeling that you do not want to let the Regiment down. It is a family Regiment, in which many members of the same family may serve at the same time. The basis which supports its confidence in itself is an amalgam of major achievements and minor but significant detail. The Black Watch is proud of its status as the senior Highland Regiment and of its long list of battle honours; it is also proud that it wears square-cut spats, and not the round-toed spats worn by all the other Scottish regiments. These links with the past are consciously and proudly remembered. The soldiers are called to meals by pipe calls such as 'Brose and Butter'. Once a month the Regiment, like the Suther-land Highlanders (the 93rd) and the Queen's Own Cameron Highlanders (the 79th) with which they composed the Highland Brigade under General Sir Colin Campbell (of Glasgow High

School) in the Crimea, is awakened by the pipes and drums in what is called the Crimean Long Reveille. Tradition says that when the Brigade was attacked by the Russians, the sentry piper, in his panic and desire to make sure that the Brigade was roused to repel the attack, played every pipe tune he knew.

To understand something of the influence with which Ernest was surrounded when he joined the Black Watch, it is necessary to know something of the Regiment's history. Its ancestry can be traced back to 1624 when the government raised Independent Companies, consisting only of Highlanders, to police the North of Scotland. The Independent Companies were further developed on 3 August 1667 when Charles II commissioned the Earl of Atholl to raise men 'to be a constant guard for securing the peace of the Highlands' and to '*watch* upon the Braes'. The main function of these forces was to prevent the 'lifting of creachs' – that is, the taking of cattle or booty. They were to arrest 'thieves' and 'broken men' and 'drivers of creachs'.

In the conditions of these times it is not surprising that the plan did not work well. The watch became venal, and tolerated rustling in exchange for payments. In effect they ran their own protection racket. They also defrauded the government by drawing pay for twice as many men as they had serving. They were not above accountancy that was more creative than accurate. In 1678 the accounts of one of the Companies shows: 'Item, for 300 baggonets for the 300 fyre locks " 2s stg *per* piece – £360.' In 1717, following the rebellion of two years earlier, the Independent Companies were disbanded and Highlanders forbidden to carry arms.

In 1724 General Wade was appointed Commander-in-Chief in Scotland. We remember him nowadays largely for the roads and bridges that he built in order to make the policing of the High-lands easier. 'If you'd seen these roads before they were made/ You'd lift up your hands and bless General Wade.' He also had a more directly military function. He re-formed six Independent Companies from loyal, Whig clans of Highlanders and allowed them to carry arms and to resume a policy of policing the Highlands. His report of that year recommended

> That Companies of such Highlanders as are well affected to His Majesty's Government be established under proper regulations, and commanded by officers speaking the language of the country, subject to martial law, and under the inspection and orders of the Governors of Fort William and Inverness, and the officer commanding His Majesty's Forces in those parts.
>
> That the said Companies be employed in disarming the Highlanders, preventing depredations, bringing criminals to justice, and hinder rebells [sic] and attainted persons from inhabiting that part of the kingdom.

In his Order of 15 May 1725 he said that officers were to find their non-commissioned officers and soldiers and that 'no man is to be listed under size of 5' 6" '. He went on to provide 'that officers commanding companies take care to provide a plaid clothing and bonnet in the Highland dress for the non-commissioned officers and soldiers belonging to their companies, the plaid of each company to be as near as they can of the same sort or colour'. Only gradually was a tartan standardised into the dark blue-black and green sett that has become famous throughout the world.

Much arcane scholarship has been deployed in identifying the source of the tartan. It seems likely that in 1725 the Black Watch adopted the tartan loosely associated with the Campbells. The Grants and the Munros do not agree.

The result of Wade's 1724 and 1725 provisions was Am Freiceadan Dubh – the Black Watch – as opposed to the red soldiers (Saighdearan Dearg) who were also stationed in the Highlands. That was, however, no more than a nickname at this stage. Officially in 1725 they were known as the Independent Highland Companies.

In 1739 George II ordered that these Companies were to be

incorporated into the Regiment of Foot, 'the men to be natives of that country [Scotland] and none other to be taken'. The Regiment, known now as the Highland Regiment, first paraded to the strength of 850 men in a field near Aberfeldy at Weem, beside the bridge that Wade had built there.

There was great enthusiasm to join the Companies. Officers and men were frequently related and the men were sometimes themselves people of some consequence with their own servants (or ghillies) to attend on them and carry their arms and baggage on the march. They joined because of the prestige that flowed from being allowed to carry arms, distinguishing them from the humiliated Highlanders to whom this badge of manliness was denied by the Disarming Acts of 1716 and 1725. The Companies were attended by pipers, dressed in the Royal Stewart tartan, and, at Wade's insistence, by drummers, whom he regarded as generating a more military noise.

The Regiment's first move out of Scotland was marked by an inauspicious incident which is still remembered with *schadenfreude* by some of its rivals. It was sent to London in 1743 on its way to Flanders and was reviewed by Wade on 14 May, the King's birthday, on Finchley Common. There was much interest in the exotic appearance of the men, which attracted crowds of spectators, but afterwards 200 Highlanders deserted and set off for home, taking their weapons and ammunition. A reward of 40 shillings *per* deserter was offered. By 18 May the deserters, under the lead of one Corporal Samuel McPherson, had reached Oundle, where they were discovered by a gamekeeper. There they dug in, but faced by cavalry they disarmed and surrendered. As they had moved away from London the Scots had been viewed with considerable fear and alarm by the English, but now that they presented no threat the apprehension turned to respect. Their progress to Oundle was compared to the March of the Ten Thousand, and Corporal McPherson was described as 'a second Xenophon'.

McPherson's men had been encouraged to throw themselves

on the mercy of the court martial that awaited them and they expected clemency. The government's reaction was however very severe: 139 men were tried for mutiny. The evidence was given in Gaelic and was translated: 79 could not speak English at all. One man, Patrick Campbell, also known as Patrick McGregor, was found not guilty because he deserted three days before the review. He got off with the lenient sentence of '1,000 lashes with a cat of nine tails upon his bare back at five different times, *vizt.*, 200 at each time'. The prisoners petitioned the court to say that they had been 'fatally impressed with an opinion that they were levied to guard the Highlands, and not to be employed elsewhere'. Their grievance was that they now found themselves being sent abroad. They might have been prepared to serve in Flanders, but feared wrongly they were to be sent to the West Indies, at which they drew the line. They strongly declared their loyalty to the Hanoverian succession. The petition was unavailing. All but Patrick Campbell were convicted and all were ordered to be shot, although only three were in the event executed. Corporal McPherson and two others were shot on Tower Hill in the presence of the Regiment. Others were dispersed to other regiments. Even the Colonel seems to have had a grudging respect for Corporal McPherson and the other two ringleaders, because he kept pictures of all three in his dining room.

Many were transported to the West Indies, which the writer of a *Short History* of the mutiny clearly regarded as worse than death. If the men were found to be undeserving of pity, he said: 'let their *fears* pronounce their *sentence*, let them not be *shot* like *soldiers*, *let them be transported* to the WEST-INDIES'. There is an unfortunate irony in the fact that they rebelled because they feared being sent to the West Indies, but would not have gone there if they had not rebelled.

Whether they had thought they were to stay in Scotland or not, the fact is that the remainder of the Regiment now went to the Continent to fight in the War of the Austrian Succession.

Although the mutiny of 1743 may not have reflected well on the

Regiment's fighting resolve, once it was abroad the martial vigour it displayed was remarked on and applauded repeatedly. The Regiment's first battle was at Fontenoy, where the soldiers were described as 'Highland Furies'. One Jock killed nine men with his broadsword.

In 1751 the Regiment received the number 'the 42nd', a designation that was to be become famous to the point of being part of Scots mythology, 'the Forty-Twa'.

Five years later the Regiment was fighting the French in America, where the Red Indians thought that they were relatives. At the Battle of Ticonderoga in 1758 half the men and two thirds of the officers were killed or wounded. One officer wrote: 'The affair at Fontenoy was nothing to it: I saw both'. At this time the title Royal was conferred on the Regiment and a second battalion was raised. The Regiment was slowly assuming its identity: in 1768 it adopted more or less its present badge, and its motto: *'Nemo Me Impune Lacessit'*.

By 1776 the Regiment was back in America, this time to fight the Americans. It is interesting to note the time spent in travel in these years: when it returned to Portsmouth in October 1789, it set off to march to Tynemouth in Northumberland, which took it about a month. It would be done within the day by train nowadays. It stayed put at Tynemouth through the winter months when travel on the roads was difficult and moved on in the spring to Berwick, Edinburgh and Glasgow. Then back to Edinburgh for winter. It only reached the Highlands the following spring.

During the Napoleonic wars the Regiment spent much time in Flanders, as it was to do rather over 100 years later. Legend has it that it was at one of the battles there, at Geldermalsen, that it was awarded its Red Hackle. There is doubt about this, but on the Regiment's return from this campaign there was an issue of red feathers, and the army order of 20 August 1822 safeguarded the right to wear a 'Red Vulture Feather in its bonnets . . . to be used exclusively by the 42nd Regiment'. It seems likely that the hackle dates in fact from the time of the Regiment's service in America.

After Flanders the 42nd saw further service during the Napoleonic wars in the West Indies, at the capture of Menorca and in Egypt. There was a famous incident in 1801 at the Battle of Alexandria when the Regiment was under attack from the crack French battalion 'The Invincibles'. General Abercrombie magnificently called out: 'My brave Highlanders, remember your country, remember your forefathers!' Every man stood firm, though Abercrombie himself died of a wound sustained in the battle. Sir John Fortescue, the author of *The History of the British Army*, wrote of the Regiment in this battle: 'The 42nd stand pre-eminent for a gallantry and steadfastness which will be difficult to match in the history of any army'. Here the Regiment won the honour of bearing the Sphinx with the word EGYPT as a badge on its colours.

The 42nd was at Corunna. General Moore, who was a Scot and an admirer of the Regiment and its hardihood, moved around the perimeter line from which the forces were famously to withdraw and addressed them: 'Highlanders, remember Egypt!' It was while he was watching the 42nd withdraw that he suffered the hit that was to kill him. A soldier from the Regiment helped him behind a wall and six others carried him back.

There were many other engagements before the end of the Napoleonic wars. At Quatre Bras, as at Alexandria, the Regiment appeared to be facing impossible odds. French officers shouted: 'Why don't you surrender? Down with your arms! You see you are beaten'. It was in fact the French who withdrew, although the 42nd lost their commanding officer, two other officers, forty men and many wounded.

The 42nd played a part at Waterloo but there were then forty years before further action, when the Regiment was in the Crimea as part of the Highland Brigade. Sir Colin Campbell was so proud of his Brigade that he asked for and was granted permission to wear a feather bonnet like his men. A special hackle was made up for him, the top one third red for the 42nd, and the remainder white for the other Regiments. It was he in the Crimea who used the famous words, 'Forward the 42nd!', that became part of Scottish lore.

The Black Watch was in India at the Mutiny when a princely gong was appropriated which has ever since been struck to mark the hour and half-hour throughout the daylight hours wherever the Regiment is stationed.

It was only in 1861 that Queen Victoria authorised the official use of the name 'The Black Watch' in addition to the other names of the Regiment. During the Ashanti War there was another of those incidents that become the stuff of regimental history and prestige. Colonel McLeod, in charge of the advance guard, asked to be reinforced by his own Regiment, which had suffered severely in an earlier battle and was being held in reserve. The Regiment came forward exhausted and in some disarray after a quick march. Colonel McLeod displayed remarkable self-discipline and control. He was determined that the Regiment should not be deployed until it was absolutely ready. To everyone's amazement he ordered 'Markers Out' and as the Commander-in-Chief, Sir Archibald Allison, writing in the third person, recalled,

formed the 42nd into a most accurate parade line, which he corrected and dressed till it stood as firm and motionless as if it had been awaiting an inspection at Aldershot. Sir Garnet Wolseley, and even Sir Archibald Allison, began to be impatient of the delay, especially as the enemies' bullets were humming through the trees, but the experienced Scottish warrior would not move until his trusty battalion was absolutely in hand, and showed no sign of bustle. Then only did he give the order to advance . . . 'Pipes to the heads of companies,' and well knowing the tremendous effect of the British shout, 'The men will cheer.'

Then such an exciting episode was seen as stirred the blood and called forth the admiration of the spectators. The companies wheeled off, the skirl of the pipes roused the Scotsmen to a fury, and, like a disciplined avalanche, they rushed forward . . . Such and so determined a movement could not but be victorious. In the words of Sir Archibald's own despatch, 'without stop or stay the 42nd rushed on, cheering, their pipes blowing, their officers to the front;' ambuscade after ambuscade was carried, village after village won in succession, till the whole Ashanti broke and fled in the wildest order down the road to Coomassie.

In 1881 the Cardwell reforms required that each Regiment should have two battalions, one abroad and one at home. The 42nd was linked with the 73rd. This was not an unnatural marriage, as the 73rd had been the 42nd's original second battalion in 1779. All the same, different traditions and different cultures had developed and it was some time before the marriage was a happy one. The 73rd had its own distinguished history at Seringapatan, Pondicherry, Mysore, Quatre Bras and Waterloo. In 1852 there had occurred a famous incident that became a cherished and emotional part of the Victorian heritage. A draft of men including men of the 73rd were on their way to the Cape on HMS *Birkenhead,* an early paddle steamer, when it struck a rock in Simons Bay just east of Cape Town, and broke its back. The men were drawn up on deck and told by the ship's officers that their only chance was to jump overboard and swim for the boats. But their own officers then said that this would imperil the chances of women and children who were already in the boats. The men stood firm in their ranks as the ship sank: 357 were drowned, 56 of them from the 73rd, more than from any other regiment.

The episode made a huge impression on the Victorian psyche. The German Emperor was so impressed that he caused an account of the event to be read out to every Regiment in his army on three separate parades. The order, 'Women and Children First', originates from the example of the stoic discipline of the soldiers, and the expression, 'the Birkenhead Drill', found its way into the national thesaurus, meaning standing firm, facing certain death, so that weaker ones may have a chance to live. Kipling, as so often, provided the words that people would remember:

To stand and be still
To the Birkenhead Drill
Is a damn tough bullet to chew.

The episode of the *Birkenhead*, however, did more than inspire Kipling and generate a new tradition when a ship went down: it formed one of those imperial vignettes which impressed itself on the mind of Victorian Britain, and with so many others incrementally formed the outlook of the young men of 1914.

The united Regiment was active in many spheres, including Tel-el-Kebir, the Sudan, India and South Africa. At Magersfontein, in 1889, 301 out of 943 personnel were killed or wounded, including 17 of 27 officers.

In addition to the two regular battalions of the Regiment there were by the time of the First World War also Volunteer Reserve units. The first of these units traces its roots to the Perthshire Militia, which was set up in 1798 as a volunteer force opposing the threat of Napoleonic invasion. It was subsumed in 1803 into the Royal Perthshire Militia. That unit in turn was officially disbanded but unofficially continued in being, repeatedly offering its services to the nation. It made itself available to its country at the time of the Crimea, the Indian Mutiny, the 1882 war in Egypt. In each case its services were declined. But finally the Third Militia Battalion, the Black Watch, was embodied in 1899 and sent out drafts to the Second Battalion. The Haldane reforms meant that recruits were, as they had not previously been, obliged to accept service abroad. By the time the First World War broke out the Third Militia Battalion was well established at Nigg in Ross-shire. The 4th, 5th, 6th and 7th battalions were Territorial Army units, organised in terms of the same reforms. Ernest was to be commissioned into the 3rd Battalion; the 9th, to which he would later be attached, did not exist when the First World War broke out.

Originally the 42nd was an entirely Highland unit. As the years went by this tradition continued but was diluted. The 73rd had also started as a Highland unit but lost that connection relatively soon. By the time of the amalgamation of the 42nd and 73rd, most men in the amalgamated unit were not Highlanders, but remained Scottish. The Regiment was still regarded as being a Highland unit – as it frequently still is – but after the Cardwell reforms the Regimental area became the Counties of Angus, Fife and Perthshire. The Scottish, if not the Highland, connection was, however, unassailable and even by the Second World War four-fifths of the men were Scottish.

The following extracts from the Standing Orders and Regulations 1906, issued at Fort George on 27 November 1905, give some idea of the culture of the Regiment:

In publishing a new edition of standing orders for the use of the Regiment Colonel A. G. Duff directs they shall take the place of any others. It should be the first duty of everyone to maintain the heritage and high standard of discipline which is the birthright of our Regiment.

The Officers of the Regiment are to encourage their men to amuse themselves at all manly games such as cricket, football etc. Money is seldom given as prizes but rather any other description of premiums which may be thought fit.

The duties of the Master Cook are so important and multifarious that there is not space to enumerate them all. He should be strenuously active and unceasing in initiative in order to ensure the men's meals being raised to the highest possible standard.

He should never let himself think that there is any limit to his power for good in this vital matter.

He is responsible that all dripping saved is handed into store and must obtain the signature of either the Quartermaster or Quartermaster Sergeant in his book for the amount handed over.

Sobriety, cleanliness in his person and the neatness of his dress ought always to be the distinguishing mark of a N.C.O. He is to assist the men by his advice and instructions whenever necessary but is never to drink or associate familiarly with them.

The Provost Sergeant will frequently visit the canteen and interfere to prevent drunkenness or riot.

To perform his duties well and agreeably to himself a private soldier should be possessed of zeal and a love for the service and in general he should be keenly alive to the character and credit of the corps he serves in; and should always recollect that disgrace or dishonour cannot fall on any individual in it without it in some degree reflecting upon the whole.

Sobriety is the first and best security against all irregularities or deviations from military discipline and drunkenness never can be admitted as an excuse for any crime a man may have been guilty of.

Dancing is recommended as a pleasant way of passing long evenings and having the advantage of pipers in the Regiment may be often resorted to: it keeps up good humour and health, and what is infinitely of more consequence, prevents the men from passing their idle hours in the canteen where habits of drunkenness and other vices are frequently contracted.

When on the line of march if a soldier finds it necessary to fall out he is to apply for leave to a Sergeant who will report to the Captain or officer in charge when a N.C.O. is to be sent with him who will be answerable that no unnecessary delay takes place in his rejoining his company.

This indulgence is to be rarely granted and indeed can very seldom be called for as all parties of the Regiment (small or great) on the line of march are to have 5 minutes at the end of every hour: such halts however are not to be in the vicinity of a public house.

Officers commanding companies are held strictly responsible for the fitting of the men's shoes, on which depends the efficient marching of the Regiment. Men should be cautioned against wearing new shoes on long marches.

The men must be taught to pay particular attention to their

dress, which will beget a feeling of self-pride very conducive to their general good conduct and as in Highland Regiments so much depends on the manner and taste of each individual in arranging the different articles of dress this is the more essentially necessary.

The high reputation they have so justly gained may be chiefly attributed to the esprit de corps, which has always belonged to them, and attention to these particulars of dress will greatly contribute to keep it alive.

The bonnet will be ten inches high with four foxtails hanging in a general slope from six inches in length below the binding for the front tail to eight inches for the rear tail. The front tail is to be in rear of the right eye: the hackle, which should not reach above the bonnet, should be exactly above the left ear. Thirty inches of ribbon forming a tie eleven inches long will be placed over the opening at the rear of the bonnet: a rosette of silk ribbon three inches in diameter will be placed below the badge.

The kilt will be made with 7 yards of tartan: the number of pleats will not be less than 26 (unless the check of the tartan exceeds 7 inches as does the Royal Stuart). It will be worn so that it reaches the centre of the knee-pan care being taken that the lower ends of the aprons coincide. Three black-headed pins are to be used for fastening and care must be taken that they are not passed through the pleats but through the body of the kilt.

The sporran is to be worn so that the top fits closely into the pit of the stomach, with the strap passing along the groins: the buckle of the strap should be in the centre of the back with the spare end to the right. The general tendency is to wear the sporran too low. Cutting of the strap is forbidden. Any alterations or punching of holes are to be done by the master shoemaker. The spare end of the strap should be not less than four inches.

The upper tassels will be arranged so that the upper points

of the leather tips are one and a half inches from the bottom edge of the sporran head; the bottom tassels with bottom edges of the leather tips exactly level with the bottom of the upper tassels.

The tone of the Standing Orders is interesting: there is a familial approach, and a paternalistic sense of responsibility to the men. The pride in the Regiment is evident, as is the desire to maintain high traditions and in particular the *esprit de corps*. That *esprit*, which both flows from and is responsible for the honours that the Regiment has won, is the compound result of many factors: it is partly the product of the Regiment's historical roots, partly the product of its fury in battle, partly its Scottishness and partly the sense of separateness from the mainstream of the British army that the history and the Scottishness have engendered.

This was the *esprit* and these were the influences that Ernest was to meet when he joined the Regiment. These were the traditions and this was the ethos that animated the Regiment throughout the First World War, in which 25 Black Watch battalions served. More than 40,000 men served in these battalions, of whom 8,000 were killed and over 20,000 were wounded. Before the war the Regiment had won 20 Battle Honours. They received a further 69 for their actions in that war, together with a further four Victoria Crosses.

6

Laurelled Armies

WITH THE THIRD BATTALION

The family that Ernest found himself with after his time at the Stirling School of Instruction was a fairly aristocratic one. The Third (Special Reserve) Battalion, the direct descendant of the Royal Perthshire Militia Regiment of Foot which had originally been embodied in Perth in 1798 to counter the Napoleonic threat, was conscious of its origins, and the list of its officers in August 1914 reads like a roll call of local dignitaries. Amongst 19 officers there was a baronet and two Honourables as well as four gentlemen with splendidly double-barrelled names. The Battalion was mobilised at Perth on 8 August, over 1,200 strong, and entrained that evening for its war station. The mobilisation station for the Battalion had originally been Devonport. That was changed in 1912 to Dover, both of these stations reflecting the prevalent concern about a German landing on the south coast, but on mobilisation, orders were received to join the Brigade which was being formed for the defence of Cromarty, and it was to Nigg in Ross-shire that the train headed on the night of 8 August. The significance of the destination was that until Scapa Flow in Orkney was fully defended, the Cromarty Firth, which contained the important base of Invergordon, was the major harbour for the British Home Fleet. The Firth is a deep indentation on the north-east coastline of Scotland, just north of Inverness. It is entered through a narrow gut to the north of the town of Cromarty. The gut is commanded on each side by the Sutor Forts. Once through the gut, warships were safe from both weather and enemy navies. But if the forts fell into the hands of the Germans, ships in the lagoon of the Firth could not escape to sea. With the Battalion in the Brigade that was defending Cromarty were 3rd Scottish Rifles, also to be stationed at Nigg for the defence of the North Sutor Fort, 3rd Seaforth Highlanders, to be stationed at Cromarty to defend the South Sutor Fort and 3rd Cameron Highlanders to be stationed at Invergordon to provide guards for naval oil tanks. Since the Germans never did invade Britain, or even make serious plans to do so, in the First War, this defensive activity appears slightly bizarre: but in the years before the War there had been very considerable fears of invasion. Archbishop Cosmo Gordon Lang had a peculiar nightmare which he recorded: a huge force of Germans had landed in the Channel ports and he (as Archbishop of York) and the Archbishop of Canterbury were leading a march of prelates towards the enemy, in an endeavour to induce them, by 'moral suasion', to return to Germany. Erskine Childers' *The Riddle of the Sands* is an example of the invasion phobia of these years, simultaneously reflecting a widespread preoccupation and contributing to the apprehension that conflict was ultimately inevitable.

It was envisaged that the enemy might attempt to land at Balintore, a small fishing village near Nigg, with the North Sutor Fort or Invergordon as their objective, or near Fortrose on the Moray Fifth to attack the South Sutor Fort. Originally it was the navy which was to be responsible for Cromarty, but on mobilisation the War Office took over the responsibility. The Battalion arrived at Nigg early on the morning of Sunday 9 August and camped, under canvas, on the shoulder of Nigg hill, replacing the 4th Battalion Seaforth Highlanders (a Territorial Battalion) which had already been there for three days. The Seaforths left on the afternoon of 9 August to join the Highland Division of Territorials at Bedford, one of the first Territorial Divisions to arrive in France.

The Battalion now started work on putting Nigg hill into a sound state of defence. Working parties established an elaborate system of trenches with barbed wire entanglements.

The fleet patrolled the coast daily, looking for enemy invaders. Balintore, about two miles north of the camp, was thought to be likely to be attacked because of its situation at a point where the contours of the coast would have facilitated landings. The precautions against landings, despite the fact that there was no evidence of preparations for one, seem much more rigorous and elaborate than in 1940, when all the evidence was that an invasion might reasonably be expected on a daily basis. The outpost line on the hill was guarded by night by one company, with another on duty as in-lying picket in camp. There were also guards and pickets at Balintore with examining posts on all main roads, and even by day a section with an officer was posted on the hill in telephone contact with the camp. These activities were soon scaled down and by the end of October all guards and pickets, except those at Balintore, had been withdrawn, although the trenches and barbed wire were maintained in a good state of repair.

Thereafter, the main activity of the Battalion was to train men for the Front. The first draft left for France as early as 26 August 1914. By the time of the Armistice on 11 November 1918, the Battalion had sent out about 1,200 officers and 20,000 other ranks as reinforcements for the fighting battalions of the Black Watch in all theatres of war: to France, to Mesopotamia, to the Balkans and to Egypt and Palestine. The chapter dealing with the Battalion in the Regimental history concludes thus:

The 3rd Battalion had not been called on to bear the strain of battle, nor to support the hardships of war, as had the fighting battalions of the Regiment. But the great majority of officers and men in the various theatres of war had been first trained in the 3rd Battalion, and while serving with it had been impressed with the traditions of the Black Watch.

The 3rd Battalion, and especially its Staff, may justly claim to have had some share in developing the brave spirit and feeling of comradeship that distinguished all battalions of the Black Watch throughout the Great War.

All drafts for France left direct for Étaples (which was to have sombre resonances for the Reid family). Ernest himself, when he left, did so with a brother officer and without a draft, so he was spared the experience of the training undergone at Étaples, with its infamous 'Bullring'. Étaples was distant from Boulogne, the port of disembarkation in France, by a march of 18 miles, which was the first test of the fitness of the men as they arrived in France. Étaples consisted of a tented encampment for 100,000 men. Wilfred Owen described it:

> It is a vast dreadful encampment. It seemed neither France nor England but a kind of paddock where the beasts were kept a few days before the shambles. There is a very strange look on all faces in that camp; an incomprehensible look which a man will never see in England nor currently see in any battle, only in Étaples. It was not despair or terror. It was more terrible than terror, for it was a blindfold look and without expression, like a dead rabbit's. It will never be painted and no actor will ever seize it.

Edmund Blunden recalled being at Étaples:

> Was it on this visit to Étaples that some of us explored the church – a fishing-village church – and took tea comfortably in an inn? These tendernesses ought not to come, however dimly, in my notions of Étaples. I associate it, as millions do, with 'The Bullring,' that thirsty, savage, interminable training-ground.

The men (to whom it was often 'Eatapples' or 'Heeltaps') breakfasted at 5.45 a.m. and were in the Bullring from 7 in the morning till 5.30 in the evening. They were under the command of officers and N.C.O.s, 'canaries' because of the yellow armbands they wore, who treated them with a pathological viciousness born more of a sense of guilt because they were not going to face the real dangers that their victims were, than from a desire to prepare the men for realities from which they had been sheltered at base in Britain. The

Bullring was vast, a far greater area than one would have thought necessary, an unforgiving white plateau of beaten sand, riven by deep fissures. When Queen Mary visited the Camp in 1917, she protected herself with a parasol against the sun and the bright light of the coast, but the men trained without protection. They drilled and practised unarmed face-to-face combat. They underwent bayonet training, bomb or hand-grenade drill, and were goaded by their tormentors as they sweated up hills of sand in full kit.

By 1917 these conditions led to mutiny. This has been dramatised and the central rôle given to Private Percy Toplis, 'The Monocled Mutineer'. His rôle is fiction, but the disturbances were real enough. They started when a New Zealander, Gunner A. J. Healey, had gone into town by walking across the estuary at low tide. The tide came in and Healey was unable to return by the clandestine route he had used on the way out. He was seized by the military police and locked up. When his fellow countrymen heard this, they surrounded the police hut. Stones were thrown and an attempt was made to rush the building. One of the camp police wrenched a pistol from a soldier and fired two rounds over the heads of the crowd. A shot hit a soldier standing on the fringe of a crowd of 3–4,000 men. The man, Corporal W. B. Wood, a Gordon High-lander, was fatally injured; a second bullet hit a French woman who was standing in Étaples itself.

The mood of the soldiers, who were an explosive mix of New Zealanders and Scots, was varied. Some wanted to chase the military police, who had prudently withdrawn. Others simply wanted to go into Étaples and have a drink. They charged a picket of unarmed men who were guarding a bridge, roaring with laughter, and went off to town. Another group of men collected outside the women's hostel. The women were locked in the recreation hut with instructions to sing hymns. Eventually a WAAC officer and a Red Cross nurse went out and spoke to the men, who dispersed. Vera Britten was a nurse at Étaples at the time of the mutiny.

The authorities were concerned by the breaches of discipline, the effect of which could have been serious. Étaples was a crucial base and the scene of immense concentrations of Commonwealth reinforcement camps and hospitals. It was remote from attack, except from aircraft (it was actually attacked towards the end of the war by German aircraft which, no doubt in error, fired on a Canadian hospital building, killing 66 people). In 1917, 100,000 troops were camped among the sand dunes and the hospitals, which included 11 general, one stationary, four Red Cross hospitals (one of which we will hear about later) and a Convalescent Depot; 22,000 wounded or sick men could be handled here. On 10 September a senior officer, Lieutenant-General Asser, arrived and ordered a board of enquiry. Pickets were put in place and reinforced against the possibility that the men in the camp, angered by the killing of Wood, would attempt to break out of the base again. This they did, although ultimately Brigadier Thomson, the base commandant, addressed various crowds, some composed of as many as 1,000 men, and persuaded them to return to the camp. The disturbances continued for several days. The men were able to move fairly easily from camp to town, the pickets showing little enthusiasm for stopping them. The rioters would go right up to the pickets until those in front were pushed on to the bayonets of the two ranks that confronted them, the front rank kneeling, with rifles loaded and bayonets ready. The picket had to put up their bayonets to avoid wounding the rioters, who pushed them aside and went through the guard.

Ultimately a substantial counterforce was assembled, with 2,000 infantry and other specialist personnel, and the series of disturbances speedily came to an end. There were courts martial and one man, Corporal Robert Short, 24th Northumberland Fusiliers, was shot for his part in the events.

The reaction of the authorities was interesting. Red flags had been flown, although probably because they had been conveniently pilfered from a railway signal hut rather than for their political significance. Haig, however, said that, 'Some men with Republican ideas got amongst [the drafts], raised red flags and made a disturbance. [The dockers] are said to be very Republican'. There were no dockers at Étaples. Haig saw links between what had happened at Étaples and the Russian February Revolution and the mutinies in the French Army, and he certainly read too much into events. His attitude is illustrative of the Establishment's fears of Bolshevism and republicanism at this time.

The miasma that hangs over Étaples is so dark and heavy that it seems appropriate that to the camp's piggeries has been traced the source of the terrible influenza pandemic of October/November 1918. In 1916 the virus spread from the animals to the soldiers and on, round the world, from central Europe to Western Samoa. Forty per cent of the population of the globe was affected, and up to 40 million people died, far more than were killed by the War. The pigs finally did more damage than the canaries.

Training at Nigg was much more humane and purposeful. The Battalion increased in strength: despite the transfers to France, large drafts of ex-soldiers and untrained men arrived daily from Perth in these early months of the war. The Battalion remained under canvas until the end of November 1914, by which time something described as 'almost a tin town' had been erected. By Christmas the whole Battalion was comfortably housed, and training could be improved. It would be unfair to think of the officers of the Battalion as akin to the canaries of Étaples who remained permanently at the base. Many of the 3rd Battalion officers went to France, to fight and die. Some officers (many wounded amongst them) also came back from France and were able to instruct with the authority of veterans who had been under fire. A routine developed, and the Battalion was formed on the basis of nine companies. Six of these were filled with recruits, two with Expeditionary Force men ('Old Contemptibles') who only remained a few weeks with the Battalion, and one company was maintained for Home Service men. In the last three weeks of their training all recruits and all fit Expeditionary Force men were formed into a training company and given a special course of instruction. A weekly return was sent from the Battalion indicating the number of men available for reinforcement of the army in France; usually the whole number was called for.

As fighting in France developed into the trench warfare that was to be the norm for the rest of the war, training became more intensive. The War Office designed a syllabus of twelve weeks' training, which was what the average recruit received. Specialist officers paid periodical visits of inspection. Each came with a bee in his bonnet, convinced, as the Regimental History says, that only '*his* speciality could win the war, be it bombing, bayonet fighting, musketry or physical drill'. Bayonet fighting courses were erected, a rifle range was constructed and systems of trenches were dug to represent a front line with communicating support trenches. The bombers practised daily from these trenches.

Ernest spent almost exactly a year here. In the OTC at university he would already have undergone extensive training in Glasgow and at camps. The additional training he would require at Nigg was limited, and he remained there as an instructor and also for the purpose of the guard duty that brought the Battalion to Nigg in the first place. The Battalion was short of officers. As early as the middle of October 1914 almost every trained officer below the rank of Major had gone to France. The Regimental History emphasises the problem caused by the shortage of trained officers and non-commissioned officers, which was remedied only by the return of wounded officers and N.C.O.s. What Ernest had not experienced in the OTC was the command of men, as opposed to fellow cadets. By the time he left Nigg, he had extensive experience of that skill.

The men cannot have had much to amuse them in Ross-shire. There was a YMCA hut in camp and the Battalion had in addition its own Regimental institute and coffee shop (the latter a slightly refined facility for the Jocks). Ernest had leaves during his year at Nigg. On one of them, in October 1915, he made his will, a typically practical, Reid move, as Elsie was to find when she was taken on the first day of her honeymoon to make *her* will. He appointed Annie his executrix and left his estate to her, or failing her to Tom, and failing him also to Douglas and Ronald. His gold watch was

Ernest Reid, 1897–1917.

Victorian domesticity. Ernest's grandfather James (1812–1887), and grandmother, Jessie Fulton, surrounded by six of the eight children they would eventually have. Ernest's father, Tom, on the rocking horse, is four and here does not display his usual appearance of sober gravity. This rather attractive early photograph (1862) hints at James's growing prosperity.

Tom Reid, Ernest's father. This photograph was taken in late middle age, but even as a young man he had a mature dignity. The elegant attire was typical.

The very model of a Provincial Governor, Sir Hugh McPherson, KCIE, at the summit of his career as Governor of Bihar and Orissa. The ascent started from a thatched cottage in Castle Street, Paisley.

Hazelwood, where the whole of Ernest's life was spent until he went to war.

Paisley Grammar School. The current building in which Ernest, but not Hugh McPherson, was educated.

The Cameronians' war memorial, Kelvingrove, Glasgow. In the background is Glasgow University, which Ernest attended from autumn 1914 until he was old enough to enlist in May 1915.

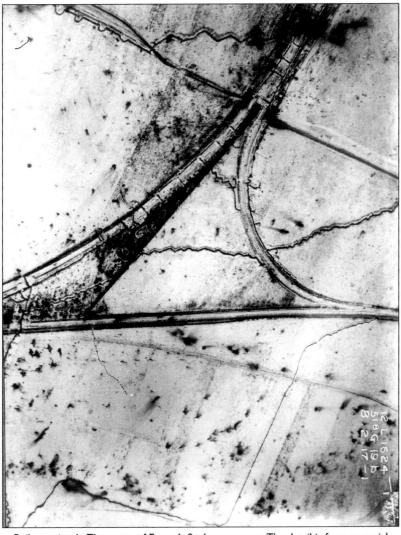

Railway triangle. The scene of Ernest's final engagement. The detail is from an aerial reconnaissance photograph taken on 8 February 1917, many weeks before the Battle of Arras, reflecting the detailed preparations that preceded operations by this stage of the war. The trenches shown in the photograph reveal how the ground had already been fought over before 1917.

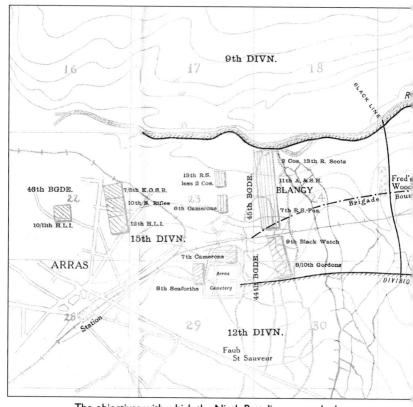

The objectives with which the Ninth Battalion was tasked
for the first day of the Battle of Arras.

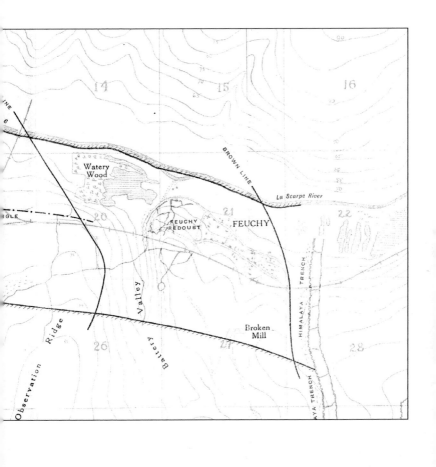

Before the Battle of Arras, 8 April 1917. Fixing scaling ladders in trenches.
Imperial War Museum, London

The Battle of Arras. Infantry getting out of an assembly trench as their wave moves
forward, 9 April 1917. *Imperial War Museum, London*

The Battle of Arras. British troops in German trenches at Feuchy, 9 April 1917.
Imperial War Museum, London

The Battle of Arras. A wounded Scottish officer and his orderly with German helmets,
10 April 1917. Echoes of Ernest and Private Black. *Imperial War Museum, London*

The Battle of Arras. Wounded men receiving refreshments from RAMC personnel at Feuchy crossroads before going on to a clearing station. On 9 April 1917 the Ninth Battalion was charged with capturing and holding the German defence line just to the east of the village. Ernest never reached that line. *Imperial War Museum, London*

The Duchess of Westminster's Hospital (British Red Cross), Le Touquet.
Imperial War Museum, London

Alexander Black, DCM, MM, the man who did so much for Ernest after he was hit.

Ernest's grave (Grave A 192) in the Military Cemetery at Étaples,
soon after it was dug.

Monchy-le-Preux, the village for which Ernest's last battle was fought.

The Military Cemetery, Étaples, 1990s.

Ernest's gravestone in the Military Cemetery at Étaples.

left to Tom. The will was signed in Tom's office at 47 Moss Street, Paisley, in the presence of two of his typists, who acted as witnesses. Making a will as a practical, commonsense measure is one thing; for Ernest, and perhaps particularly for Tom, it must have been heartbreaking to think that in all likelihood the will would be required very soon.

At some stage during his time with the 3rd Battalion, Ernest was at Strathpeffer, and he may have been billeted in what is still an elegant town and was a fashionable spa in Edwardian and Victorian times.

Early in 1916 the focus for invasion fears in Scotland moved from Cromarty to Fife, with the Forth Bridge and Rosyth Dockyard as the attractions. The Battalion, as part of the Cromarty Brigade, received orders for reinforcing a defence line which was to be held by troops from Fife and the Lothians. The Battalion was thereafter on six hours' notice of entraining. They never did have to board their trains for Fife, but four months after Ernest had left the 3rd Battalion, the unit moved from Nigg to Ireland, where the situation had become tense since the Easter Rising in 1916. One concern was the loss of many rifles from the reserve battalions of Irish regiments, taken by recruits who deserted with their equipment and arms. Conditions in Ireland were not initially ideal for training, but one positive point was, as the Regimental History puts it, that, 'owing . . . to the hostile attitude of the Highlanders towards the natives of the country, there was very little chance of any traffic in arms taking place'. Later the Battalion moved to the Curragh, where facilities were better. The Sinn Fein Movement, at the same time, spring 1918, became stronger, allegedly because of the retreat of the allied troops in the face of the Ludendorff offensive in France. 200,000 yeomanry troops were converted into cyclists and formed into a mobile brigade which was capable of moving to any part of the country at a few hours' notice. The Battalion was posted to this Brigade, and although its weekly exercise with the brigade interfered with training of the recruits, their rôle was welcomed by the men, 'especially those who had been in France and who were only too anxious to fight the Sinn Feiner, whom they considered as much an enemy as the German'.

Ernest would not have felt that chasing Irishmen was what he had volunteered for, and he had left the 3rd Battalion while it was still at Nigg: in July 1916 he received orders to proceed to France, where he was to be attached to the 9th Battalion. He received embarkation leave and then headed for London, the Channel ports and France. He had wanted to fight the Germans since the war began on 4 August 1914. He had trained for that purpose with the OTC. He had applied for a commission as soon as he was old enough. He had spent a year in Ross-shire as part of the real army, gaining the experience of command. Now he was to go to the wars.

7

Heroes! – for Instant Sacrifice Prepared

THE NINTH BATTALION. LOOS

When he left the 3rd Battalion, it was to the 9th Battalion that Ernest was attached. He joined a unit that had only been set up after the outbreak of war and in its brief history had been subjected to experiences that would have tested the morale of even the most hardened troops. The 9th Battalion was a 'Service Battalion', one of the formations that composed Kitchener's New Armies. The speed with which these bodies could be turned from gaggles of enthusiastic but unequipped and untrained volunteers into respectable fighting forces is one of the great triumphs of the First World War.

Kitchener was more than the great poster of Margot Asquith's savage description. Though his stock was to fall steadily in the eyes of his colleagues, if not in those of the general public, to such an extent that they were probably relieved when he went down with the *Hampshire* (wearing his Burberry) in June 1916, he was one of the few people in August 1914 who appreciated the likely scale and length of the war. If Churchill ensured that Britain's navy was ready when war broke out, Kitchener ensured that Britain had an army with which she could continue the war.

Immediately on his appointment as Secretary of State for War on 5 August 1914, he declared that the country must be prepared for a war that would last three years and that this would require an Army of 70 Divisions. On 6 August he wrote on half a sheet of foolscap the historic instructions for the raising of the New Armies, 'K.1', 'K.2' and so forth. The Territorial forces were

primarily required for home defence and could not be sent
abroad without parliamentary sanction, although in reality the
Territorial soldiers flocked to enlist, whole units volunteering
for service abroad. Kitchener decided that the army had to be
increased by 100,000 men, and although the units that he raised
were known as 'New Armies' at the time and have been ever
since, his scheme was not in fact to raise armies that were new,
but to add to what already existed. On 21 August 1914 Army Order
382 authorised the raising of that number of soldiers. The target
had been reached in just three days, by 24 August, and a second
100,000 was immediately authorised, followed by a third two
days later, and then a fourth.

The instructions for formation of the additional formations
(K.2 to K.4) reached Perth in September 1914. The Black Watch's
first Service Battalion, the 8th Battalion, was established by
3 September. On 6 September a further draft of 200 men left
Perth for Aldershot, and this draft is regarded as the embryo of
the 9th Battalion, which Ernest joined some 18 months later.

In that brief period the 9th Battalion had been transformed
from an assembly of unarmed civilians into a disciplined fighting
force, and had been blooded and almost broken in battle. On
9 September sanction was obtained to form the drafts which
had followed the 8th Battalion to Aldershot between 6 and 9
September into a separate unit. It was commanded by Colonel T.
O. Lloyd who had served for many years in the Regiment but had
retired in 1909. He was not the only older officer, commissioned
and non-commissioned. Although the Battalion was up to full
strength within a few days, there were very few non-commissioned officers available apart from one or two retired N.C.O.s
who had been too old to be called up for the Reserve Battalion.
Amongst the officers, apart from the commanding officer and the
quartermaster, there were only a few second lieutenants. Colonel
Lloyd had to look to another veteran for the important position of
Regimental Sergeant-Major, in G. D. Benson. Benson had left the
Regiment as far back 1902, when he was discharged to take his

pension after no less than 29 years' service during which he had received a medal for the Egyptian campaigns in 1882–85, with five clasps and the Khedive's Star. The second lieutenants who filled the mess had almost no military experience at all.

So far as the men were concerned, it was generally reckoned that the Second Army was composed of better volunteers than the First, simply because the latter had been accepted very fast indeed, with little screening. Conversely, the First Army received the primary allocations of equipment and material, so that the Second Army was very badly supplied and endured discomforts and hardships from which the First Army had been sheltered.

The régime was very hard: ten hours a day for seven days a week were spent in training. The men were remarkably enthusiastic but their uniforms were so unimpressive that many were not allowed out of barracks. This does not seem to have affected their spirits, and it was noticeable that at Aldershot the soldiers were so anxious to learn their craft that there was almost no crime in the Division of which the 9th Battalion was a part: the 15th (Scottish) Division.

The discomfort was very real. The troops were crowded into quarters that were far too small, with only one blanket or a piece of tweed apiece and without mattresses. The feeding was poor and it was fortunate that the weather at least was good in these early weeks. A brigadier wrote at the time: 'After a certain amount of weeding out – owing to lax medical inspection on enlistment – the men were splendid. Quite the pick of the new forces. The finest material I ever saw. One company (6th Camerons, 45th Brigade) was entirely composed of men from the Glasgow University and High Schools, a shocking waste of good officer material'. Another brigadier confirmed that the men of the Second Army were physically better than their predecessors, and high standards of selection were imposed to the extent that men rejected by the Second Army were later accepted in other formations.

By 26 September 1914 the Division was paraded for the first time as a formed unit and inspected by the King. With the exception of the Staff and a few senior officers, the whole Division was in plain clothes. 'Some wore straw hats, others caps and bowlers. Men clad in well-cut serge suits stood next to others in workmen's clothes but never did a body of recruits, small or large, with so little training to their credit, stand as steadily as did the 15th Division on that occasion,' reported the authors of the history of the Division, Colonel Stewart and John Buchan, in the unfailing tone of bright optimism which frequently throws their judgement into question. Buchan, a supporter of Haig, who had gone to his College at Oxford, believed in and approved of Britain's involvement in a morally good war.

The matter of clothes became rapidly more serious, and in an attempt to deal with their 'Dad's Army' appearance, the men were allowed ten shillings (50p) each towards the cost of obtaining good suits, boots and greatcoats from home: it was only towards the end of September that the first consignment of army clothing arrived. Even this hardly improved matters: the clothes that were issued consisted of English-pattern trousers and red serge jackets, some of them made as far back as 1893. One man was heard to say that he had come to be a Gordon Highlander and not a postman. A man in the Camerons said, ' A few of us made the best of a bad job by purchasing glengarries and badges to show that we belong to a Highland Regiment and not to a Red Alsatian Band'. By the middle of October the Battalion was at last dressed alike, but civilian greatcoats were retained for a long time. In the same month, donations from generous friends allowed the Battalion to purchase pipes and drums to help them on route marches, and at last on 20 and 21 January 1915 the Battalion was issued with kilts in the Black Watch tartan. On the following day the kilts were worn for the first time when the Battalion, with the rest of the Division, was inspected by Kitchener and the French War Minister, M. Millerand. The only weapons available were obsolete drill rifles supplemented by a few modern ones. There were only enough to arm the front ranks and M. Millerand was heard to say to Lord Kitchener, 'I see they have very few rifles'. M. Millerand must have been eagle-eyed: the weather was so appalling that the inspection lasted no more than ten minutes, after which the half-frozen troops marched back to billets. The 9th Battalion covered 28 miles that day, the return journey through mud and slush; but only three men fell out.

Khaki tunics and military greatcoats were issued a few days later, and the Battalion was now at last properly clad in the uniform of the Black Watch, nearly five months after its formation.

Training continued in and around Aldershot and then later near Swindon. Musketry practice had to be carried out with only 25 service rifles for the whole Battalion; bayonet training was presumably carried out with equal difficulty. Nonetheless bayonet training did take place, and rifle training, and the Battalion passed Table A and Table B. Training of specialists, such as signallers and machine-gunners, was carried out with particular difficulty because of lack of equipment. Lewis-gunners had to learn their drill with wooden models and the signallers knocked together anything they could in the shape of a telephone or telegraph instrument. The wooden dummy Lewis-guns were not replaced with real ones until summer. The material deficiencies experienced by troops in training in the early part of the Second World War are well known, but it is now forgotten that the deficiencies in the materials of war were at least as great in the early years of the First War. When the Battalion moved to Chiseldon Camp, for instance, they were accommodated in some comfort in good huts, but the contractors had forgotten to build roads within the camp so that the ground round the huts and the parade ground itself were no more than a sea of mud. A company diary of March 1914 reports:

> The state of the company, owing to the mud, is such that it almost excluded the possibility of getting the men out of the huts now that they are in them.

In May Kitchener again inspected the Brigade and in the following month the King also carried out a second review: the ceremonial march past was achieved without ever having been practised beforehand. Nevertheless, the Battalion History, which was written by serving officers and, unlike the Divisional History, is remarkably sober and objective, records that 'fully equipped and ready to take the field, it [the Battalion] was a very different formation to that which His Majesty had last seen in September 1914, and anyone not closely associated with it would have had difficulty in believing that such a change could have been effected in so short a time'.

A general leave was granted and embarkation orders were issued on Sunday 4 July. The King communicated the following message just before the Battalion set off from Folkestone on the SS *Invicta* for Boulogne:

> Officers, non commissioned officers and men of 15th Division.
>
> You are about to join your comrades at the Front, in bringing to a successful end this relentless War of eleven months' duration.
>
> Your prompt patriotic answer to the Nation's call will never be forgotten. The keen exertion of all ranks during the period of training has brought you to a state of efficiency not unworthy of my Regular Army. I am confident that in the Field you will nobly uphold the traditions of the fine Regiments whose names you bear.

When the Battalion reached Boulogne, it made its way to Ostremond Camp, where, as part of the 44th Brigade, it settled briefly on the site of the camp from which Napoleon had contemplated an invasion of England. It moved on to experience billeting in France. The Commanding Officer, second-in-command and adjutant were lodged in the chateau of a M. Du Pont, who, with his wife, courteously did everything he could to make them comfortable. When he was thanked on the eve of departure, he replied that it was nothing, adding with *politesse, 'C'est pour nous sauver que vous êtes venus'*.

With little delay the Battalion moved into the trenches and experienced for the first time the reality of war in France.

These realities do not seem to have distressed the Battalion very much. They were more shaken by an order from the Brigade commander, who said that the Red Hackle was too conspicuous to be worn when the Battalion was in the trenches:

Here was a serious situation. Never had a Battalion of the Regiment ever gone into action without [the Red Hackle] since its award in 1795. Fortunately Colonel Lloyd dined with the Divisional Commander [General McCracken] on 15 [August] and took the opportunity of explaining what the 'Red Hackle' meant to every Black Watch man, and on hearing this General McCracken immediately withdrew his veto. By 12 September every man in the 9th Battalion was issued with a Hackle which was always worn until the adoption of the steel helmet precluded its continuance while in the trenches.

The experiences of the Battalion were not untypical of those of most units on the Western Front at this time until the Battle of Loos, in September 1915.

The Battalion reached France a year after the outbreak of the Great War. At the outset of the War both sides were confident that the conflict would not last long. Speed was implicit in the strategy of both the major antagonists. Germany's moves were based on the Schlieffen Plan, which involved a swift flail through Belgium, 'the last man's sleeve brushing the Channel'. French strategy had its origins in 'Plan 17', a dash across the Rhine. In the event neither Plan worked as was intended or was fully implemented.

Even so, in the first two months of the war there *was* movement: jostling round Paris, cavalry charges, fluidity. At the Battle of the Marne, British cavalry was sometimes forty miles beyond the German front line. But by the end of October, and the First Battle of Ypres, the flaw in Great War planning had been revealed: defence was easier than attack. Trenches were dug, and the war settled into stalemate.

The establishment of the trenches is never referred to without saying that they ran from Switzerland to the sea. So they did, but although trench warfare continued without cease from now until November 1918, that does not mean that it took place along the whole length of the Front. On substantial sections of the line a tacit truce persisted throughout the War, each side leaving the other more or less in peace; or disturbed only occasionally, for form's sake. On most sections, however, and for most of the time, there was regular if intermittent activity: sniping and shelling, and nocturnal raids designed to gather intelligence or simply to maintain the offensive spirit.

And each year of the war was marked by a series of great offensives, the 'Battles' of the Great War, which were designed to achieve the breakthrough that was to bring the conflict to an end, but which Lloyd George, an intemperate critic of the military commanders, characterised collectively as 'the ghastly butchery of a succession of vain and insane offensives'. It was in these infernal onslaughts that so many young lives were lost, so many bodies and minds broken. Despite the cost of these convulsive struggles in terms of men and *matériel*, the line of the trenches scarcely moved. From the end of 1914 until the spring of 1918, the Front was almost static, a scar inflicted on the face of Europe by this unwanted monster that civilisation had inadvertently created, and that fed on the blood of youth until a generation had been destroyed.

But as 1915 opened, the generals and the politicians still thought that the War would be reasonably short. The resignation and pessimism had not set in that followed the Battle of the Somme in the following year, when many men began to see no reason why the war should not go on forever. Britain's first major effort on the Western Front in 1915 was at Neuve Chapelle. For the only time in the war she was also seriously involved elsewhere: at Gallipoli. Gallipoli was however doing nothing for occupied France (and ultimately did nothing for Britain), and at the Chantilly Conference in July, Kitchener promised Joffre that if the Gallipoli campaign were allowed to continue, Britain would launch an autumn campaign on the Western Front. As autumn approached, Joffre insisted that Britain implement her part of the bargain, and attack at Loos. Sir John French, the British Commander-in-Chief, demurred because of the unsuitable terrain, but Kitchener was concerned that Joffre might be replaced and France withdraw from the war. French was ordered to comply with Joffre's request. Thus, just as Ernest joined the 3rd Battalion, the 9th Battalion found itself at Loos.

Germany had felt able to move a number of divisions from her Western Front to the Russian Front, because she did not consider that Britain had sufficient trained men to attack in France or Flanders. The New Armies were not taken seriously. Germany would have felt particularly secure in the vicinity of Loos, which was one of the weakest parts of the Allied Front, being at the junction of the French and British lines. The tragedy of Loos was an exquisite one, like many of the Great War battles, in that not only was so much blood spilled, but victory was tantalisingly close. If the British advance had gone just a little further and had been consolidated, the Allied breakthrough would have been very significant and might have brought the war to an early end. Loos was to mark the end of French as Commander-in-Chief. Haig and others were plotting against him and Haig in particular blamed him for holding back the Reserve Division. Generals suffered along with their men at Loos. No fewer than three were killed in the battle. It is a myth that generals had a sheltered existence in the First World War: it is not the job of generals to get shot, but 78 generals were killed or died of wounds, as against about 20 in the Second World War.

Loos, a mining village near Lens, was approached by open ground that was particularly heavily defended with barbed wire. The battle began with a gas attack by the British. Gas had been used by the Germans earlier, at Ypres, and despite the moral condemnation poured on such despicable tactics, Britain did not experience much difficulty in copying them. The gas discharge did little good: some cylinders leaked, others were damaged by artillery fire, the wind changed, and in the confusion casualties were caused by 'friendly' gas. In the face of some of this confusion, there were many acts of gallantry, including that of Piper Laidlaw of the 7th KOSB who found that the men of his Battalion were nervous on account of the gas in the trenches. He jumped up on to the parapet and marched up and down playing *Scotland the Brave*, despite the rifle and machine-gun fire which was sweeping the line, and despite the gas surrounding him. Although wounded, he continued to play and encouraged his men forward and over the first two lines of German trenches. He was awarded the Victoria Cross.

The 9th Battalion was on the right of the 44th Brigade where its task was to take an enemy redoubt on the road from Loos to the very Frenchly named village of Philosophe.

It must be remembered that the unit was a new creation, composed of men who had almost all been civilians for all but the previous nine months of their lives. The unit into which these men had been welded had none of the history or traditions or *esprit de corps* that support men in an established unit. There had been little time to be taught the techniques of war. General McCracken told the men in his first lecture to the Division that there were three things which went to make a good soldier. The first was discipline, the second was discipline and the third was discipline. Now what was impressed on all ranks was, 'Keep going: a constant flow of reinforcements will be following you'. The point of Loos is precisely that this was not the case.

The test of the training that the 9th Battalion had received over these nine months came at 6.30 a.m. on 25 September. The leading two platoons of A Company leapt on the parapet and, making their way through the British wire, which had already been cut for the purpose, advanced towards the German front line followed by the remainder of the Battalion at regular intervals. The Battalion history goes on:

It seemed impossible to realise that these lines were disciplined soldiers who had been twelve short months before, almost all civilians. Perfect steadiness prevailed, regardless of the heavy fire which, coming more specially from the

'Lens Road Redoubt', swept the ground over which they had to cross. There was no shouting or hurry; the men moved in quick time, picking up their 'dressing' as if on a ceremonial parade. The distance to be crossed varied from 80 to 200 yards, and, despite the fierce fire, not a line wavered or stopped. The day after the Battalion came out of action Lieutenant Colonel, now Major-General, Sir John Burnett-Stuart, G.S.O.1, 15th Division, told Colonel Lloyd that the finest sight he had ever seen was that of the 9th Black Watch advancing on the German First Line.

One officer who witnessed the Division's assault wrote:

It was magnificent. I could not have imagined that troops with a bare 12 months' training behind them could have accomplished it. As the men reached our wire they made their way through it with perfect coolness and deliberation, in spite of the enemy's increasingly heavy rifle fire. Once in No Man's Land, they took up their dressing and walked – yes coolly walked – across towards the enemy trenches. There was no running or shouting; here and there a man finding himself out of line would double for a pace or two, look to his right and left, take up his dressing and continue the advance at a steady walk. The effect of these seemingly unconcerned Highlanders advancing upon them must have had a considerable effect on the Germans. I saw one man whose kilt had got caught in our wires as he passed through a gap. He did not attempt to tear it off, but carefully disentangling it, doubled up to his correct position in the line and went on.

Within five minutes both the German Front and Support Lines had been taken. The cost was this: three Company Commanders and four Lieutenants had been killed, together with all four Company Sergeant Majors and over 200 other ranks. Nearly all the remaining officers and a large number of the other ranks had been wounded. The last words of one of the company commanders,

Major Henderson, as he lay on the ground, were to his company: 'Keep going'.

The redoubt was captured and the Black Watch, now reinforced by the Camerons, fought their way through Loos. Just before they arrived at the village a German officer approached Second Lieutenant A. Sharpe and threw up his hands, whereupon Sharpe ordered his men not to fire on him. Immediately another German officer standing behind the first one shot Sharpe dead with his revolver.

The advance continued in increasing confusion as different battalions became intermingled so that as they approached the target of Hill 70 the 15th Division found itself exposed on both flanks. The 1st Division to the left had been held up from the outset by uncut wire and the 19th London Division on the right had not appeared. There was much heroism in the attempts to press the attack further forward and in protecting the exposed flanks, but ultimately Colonel Lloyd received a message from General Wilkinson: 'The 62nd Brigade is marching on Loos. If Hill 70 is held by us they will support and if necessary relieve the 44th Brigade'. Colonel Lloyd sent a message to the Seaforths, Gordons and Camerons: 'In view of Brigade message . . . what are your views, do you consider relief desirable?' The Colonels of the Gordons and Camerons replied that they considered relief urgent. No response was received from the Seaforths. Colonel Lloyd's reply to Brigade was inevitable. Barely 90 men remained, including Headquarters. As a whole the Brigade had lost about 75% of its total strength. A message was sent setting out the position and at midnight orders were received to the effect that the Brigade would be withdrawn on relief by the 21st Division. This took place in the early hours of 26 September when the 9th Black Watch was relieved and marched back to Philosophe where it arrived at 3.30 a.m.

The Germans were as impressed as other observers. They saw an 'entire front covered with the enemy's infantry'. They stood up, and some stood even on the parapet of the trench, and fired into the approaching wave of infantrymen as they advanced over open ground. The machine-guns were able to open fire at 1,500 yards' range. 'Never had machine guns had such straightforward work to do . . . with barrels becoming hot and swimming in oil, they traversed to and fro along the enemy's ranks; one machine gun alone fired 12,500 rounds that afternoon. The effect was devastating. The enemy could be seen falling literally in hundreds, but they continued their march in good order and without interruption.' Eventually they reached the unbroken wire of the Germans' second position. 'Confronted by this impenetrable obstacle the survivors turned and began to retire.'

The Germans were taken aback by the efficacy of their machine-guns. They called the battle the Field of Corpses of Loos, *Der Leichenfeld von Loos*. One German regimental diary commented, following the failure of a fifth British attack, as the wounded men worked their way back to the British lines, 'No shot was fired at them from the German trenches for the rest of the day, so great was the feeling of compassion and mercy for the enemy after such a victory'.

Out of a total of 940 men who went into action, only 98 returned to Philosophe that morning. The Battalion had lost 360 other ranks killed or missing and 320 wounded, together with nine officers killed and one died of wounds and 11 wounded: a total of 701 of all ranks. The Brigade was ordered on the following day to withdraw and concentrate at Mazingarbe. When it reached its area, the whole Battalion was accommodated in 'Black Watch Farm', which prior to the battle had not been big enough to take in 'A' Company on its own. 'The Birkenhead Drill / Is a damned hard bullet to chew . . . '

Brigadier-General H. F. Thuillier, later to command the Division, recorded later:

A day or two after the first attack I had occasion to pass over the ground where the 15th Division had assaulted the German trenches. In front of the remains of that work known as the 'Lens Road Redoubt' (Jew's Nose), the dead Highlanders, in

Black Watch tartan, lay very thick. In one place, about 40 yards square on the very crest of the ridge, and just in front of the enemy's wire, they were so close that it was difficult to step between them. Nevertheless the survivors swept on and through the German lines.

As I looked on the smashed and riven ground, the tangled belt of wire still not completely cut, and the swathes of dead, every man lying as he had fallen, face to the enemy, I was amazed when I thought of the unconquerable, irresistible spirit which those newly raised units of the 'New Armies' must possess to enable them to continue their advance after sustaining such losses.

Returning for Loos along the straight Lens road I met a Sergeant and six or eight men of the 7th KOSB near the top of the ridge where the old German Front Line had been. I warned the Sergeant that he would be exposed to enemy machine-gun fire further along the road, and advised him to take his men across country. He thanked me, and asked how he could get to Hill 70. I replied that he couldn't get there at all, as it was now in the enemy's hands. He evidently doubted this statement, for he said, 'How can that be, sir? The Regiment took the hill and got over the other side.' I answered that there had been a lot of fighting since then, and that the Germans were on the top of it now, and enquired why he wanted to go there so particularly. He said that his Colonel had sent him up to bury two officers of the Regiment who had been killed on the top of the Hill. I again told him that it was out of the question, but his reply was that he knew exactly where the officers had fallen, and that he and his party proposed to get as near the spot as possible by daylight, creep out at night, and bring in the bodies. I explained, or tried to, the utter impossibility of such a proceeding. His answer was, 'Well, sir, we couldn't go back and face the Regiment when we hadn't even tried to bury the officers, so we'll be getting along and make the best try we can. Thank you kindly for warning us all the same.' At these words his men, who had been listening intently throughout, gave unmistakeable murmurs of assent and the party prepared to move off. Knowing the futility of their errand, I then said, 'Now, look here, Sergeant, it's really quite useless. You'll only lose your lives and we cannot afford to lose men like you. Your spirit does you and your Regiment credit, but I am not going to allow you to go to certain death. I therefore take it on myself to forbid you to go, and order you back to your Regiment.' To this the N.C.O. replied, rather obstinately and evidently very disappointed, 'Well, sir, if you order me to go back, I must go, but I can't face the Colonel and say I haven't carried out his orders unless I show him in writing the order you have given me. I must also ask you, sir, if you will excuse me, to give me a note with your name, rank and Regiment on it.' I gave him the necessary documents, and saw him and his party, very reluctantly turn about and go down the road towards Mazingarbe.

I do not think I have ever been more impressed with the soldierly bearing and spirit of any men than I was with that of those eight or nine Scotsmen. The N.C.O. appeared to be an old Regular soldier, but his men were all youngsters.

The above account does not show the real difficulty I had in turning them from their purpose. It is a weak description of the true spirit of discipline, determination and courage, combined with loyalty and affection towards their officers, which positively shone in their words and looks. I thought at the time what a splendid Battalion it must be, of which a small detachment, far from its own officers, could carry with it such a manifestation of the true Regimental spirit. Later, in 1917, when I had the great privilege of commanding the 15th (Scottish) Division, I learnt that every Battalion was the same. I found the same spirit undestroyed by two years of hard and stubborn fighting, or by the losses which every unit had suffered in the great battles of 1915, '16 and '17.

The sergeant was a Regular, but the spirit of the volunteers of the 9th Battalion was no less professional and all the more remarkable. Major Stewart of the 9th Battalion wrote to his wife after the battle: 'The main thing is to kill plenty of Huns with as little loss to oneself as possible; it's a great game and our allies are playing it top hole'.

Amidst the bravery of the soldiers, it is worth remembering the courage of some civilians and particularly of a young girl, Mlle Emilienne Moreau, the 'Lady of Loos'. She, with her mother, brother and small sister, remained in Loos throughout the German occupation. On 25 September, after the 44th Brigade had stormed the village, she did all she could to help at the dressing station of Captain Bearn, the 9th Battalion's medical officer. She and her mother throughout the day supplied the wounded with coffee which they made in the cellar of their ruined home and she did what she could to help Captain Bearn. The dressing station had to move on three different occasions because of shellfire, and on each occasion Emilienne moved with it. In their third location, Captain Bearn and his party found they were being subjected to sniper fire from some houses opposite. They could not work out from which house the fire came. Emilienne grabbed a revolver that was lying on the table, ran out and disappeared behind the opposite houses. A few seconds later there were two shots and she returned, laid down the revolver, quietly said, '*C'est fini*', and continued her work as if nothing had happened. Later in the day Captain Bearn asked her about the episode. She took him to the back of the houses, through some gardens, up a flight of stairs and showed him the bodies of two Germans whom she had shot. The exploit was reported to General McCracken and a car was sent for Captain Bearn, who was told to find Emilienne. She was taken to Divisional headquarters and shortly afterwards received a British Military Medal, and then the Croix de Guerre with palms, and thereafter the Medals of the British Red Cross and St John Ambulance Society. Her citation reads: 'Only 17½ years of age at the time, Mlle Moreau displayed the courage of the bravest of the brave'.

The Battalion received many words of appreciation in the after-math of Loos. One gesture that seems to have been particularly welcomed occurred when Colonel Lloyd and the second-in-command were walking through Mazingarbe and the 1st Battalion passed on their way to the Front Line. Their commanding officer, Lieutenant-Colonel C. E. Stuart, stopped and on behalf of the 1st Battalion of the Regiment congratulated Colonel Lloyd on what the 9th Battalion had achieved at Loos. This was communicated to the Battalion: 'The Commanding Officer of the 1st Battalion has just been over to express to the Commanding Officer the great pride which all ranks of the 42nd feel at the splendid work of the 9th Black Watch on September 25th'. For a Service Battalion, a Battalion of amateurs, to receive this acknowledgement from a Regular Battalion of the 42nd was very special. The 15th Division received from Major-General Sir Henry Rawlinson an acknowl-edgement of the 'high appreciation of the admirable fighting spirit which they displayed in the attack and capture of Loos village and Hill 70 . . . The Major-General wishes to say that he is very proud of his Command'. Sir Douglas Haig attached his congratulations to this message. Finally, General McCracken made a speech to the Battalion on 2 October 1915 at Houchin when he said:

Colonel Lloyd, officers, non-commissioned officers and men of the 9th Battalion the Black Watch.

I have come here to say just two or three words only.

You have heard already, and everyone knows, that your behaviour during the recent operations has been much appreciated . . .

I have already heard that your people know which Division took the great part in the operations – you will have told them yourselves. If they do not know they will in the course of the next few days.

I want to add one word more. I want to impress upon you the quality which made you perform the deeds of that day.

The quality you possess is discipline. Without discipline an

Army is only a mob, but with discipline it is an instrument with which a Commander can do almost anything. You have discipline. Officers, non-commissioned officers and men should work to this end all the time.

I grieve for your losses. Remember lives that have been given up . . . in the best cause of all – fighting for their country.

Your country is proud of you.

8

Drums Beat and Trumpets Blow!

THE SOMME

In the autumn of 1915, when Ernest, still with the 3rd Battalion in Scotland, was on leave, making his will, the 9th Battalion, composed of recent civilians just like him, was taking stock of the effects of battle. What was amazing in the aftermath of Loos was the extent to which the Battalion just carried on as normal. It was not amalgamated with another battalion, as was to happen with the 4th/5th Battalion (in which, however, the 9th was ultimately subsumed in May 1918). There are hints that while the Battalion remained at Houchin for five days of reorganisation there was a sense of dismay in the face of starting again to recreate the spirit and identity that had been established during the months of preparation in England, but little time was allowed for introspection. The Battalion, with the Division, was now in Reserve and as well as being allowed to rest, it started re-training and re-equipping. *Matériel* was obtained to replace what had been lost, and specialists, such as machine-gunners (almost all of whom had been killed or wounded), signallers, runners and N.C.O.s, were selected and trained. No fewer than eighteen Second Lieutenants were brought out from the 11th Battalion in Scotland and drafts of 505 other ranks joined. At the end of this period of recruitment the Battalion was up to numerical strength but not to its former standard of efficiency. Astonishingly, however, as early as 25 September the Division was ordered to return to the Front Line in the battle which still continued round Loos. They faced nothing of the enormity of the earlier attacks on Loos and Hill 70, but did have to cope with all the horrors of trench warfare, exacerbated by particularly bad weather. On 19 November Colonel Lloyd was ordered to be evacuated sick on the recommendation of the Medical Officer. He had been suffering from sciatica, aggravated by the weather conditions that the Battalion faced. Although he hoped to return, he was not passed medically fit and never did resume his command.

At this time there appears to have been a degree of reassessment. Towards the end of October steel helmets were issued for the first time. Scottish soldiers did not regard them as a suitable military headdress and there was some difficulty in persuading even frontline sentries to wear them. They were often put to unofficial uses, such as washing-up basins, and Staff Officers, for the same reasons of personal vanity as the Jocks, continued to set a bad example by appearing in the Front Line, when they did visit it, not in steel helmets, but in 'brass' hats.

The issuing of helmets was one example of a new, more professional approach. Others were the formation of machine-gun companies within the infantry brigades, the adoption of continental time (without which liaison with Britain's allies must have been fraught with misunderstandings) and the development of the Stokes trench-mortar to counter the effects of a new and heavy weapon the Germans had developed.

More generally, there was a reappraisal of training, which now continued when units went into the line; and a systematic and intensive approach was adopted that was to develop and persist through the War. It was recognised that training was better given not in the United Kingdom, but in France, where conditions were understood and changes could quickly be devised when they were found to be necessary.

There must be a question whether this change of approach reflected a recognition that the hasty training of the New Armies in England with dummy weapons had not been enough. More broadly, how efficient were the New Armies? In the patriotic climate of the times it was scarcely ever suggested that the New

Armies were any less effective than their Regular counterparts. But it is scarcely likely that recruits with only a few months' training could have honed their professional skills. That is what the Germans assumed when they moved units to the Eastern Front against the arrival of Kitchener's Armies on the Western Front, and that their assumption was sound is suggested by the intensification of training that followed the disaster of Loos, where of nearly 10,000 British soldiers involved in the attack, 385 officers and 7,861 men were killed or wounded.

The *Official History* records that when General Haking asked survivors on the afternoon of the second day, What had gone wrong?, the men replied, 'We did not know what it was like. We will do it right next time'. It was noted that many of the young volunteers of 18 and 19 understandably reacted to their experience of the Front Line by exhibiting 'definite hysterical manifestations (mutism and tremors)'. Haig recorded in his diary on 8 October that 'Some of the wounded had gone home and said that they had been given impossible tasks to accomplish and that they had not been fed'.

And yet the training did enable the men to do what they were above all asked to do: to advance steadily across no-man's land under fire, as if on a parade-ground. Units did not crack: they behaved with a courage and steadiness and discipline of which eighteenth-century Prussian guardsmen would have been proud. If their marksmanship or speed of fire was inferior to that of seasoned troops, that was not of critical importance when they were not in defence. In attacks on the Western Front in the first years of the war infantrymen were not called upon to display great technical skills.

The New Armies did well enough what they were called upon to do. Infantry tactics on the Western Front were less important than discipline. Kitchener's recruits learned as they fought: by 1918 the New Armies were far more highly trained than in 1915 or 1916 (when the New Armies were still being described as a 'collection of divisions'). If they were never as professional as the original B.E.F., that may not be of great consequence, and they had technical skills that the old Army never had.

Looking ahead, the War was eventually lost by the Germans, when their economy and morale had broken. But they were evolving battlefield tactics learned on the Eastern Front that brought them close to victory in 1918 and were again to do so in the blitzkrieg of 1940. What they used were combined arms squads: not just riflemen, but machine-gunners, mortar-operators, grenadiers and flamethrower troops, including only a few riflemen. Such troops, supported by perfected, rolling, heavy artillery barrages and gas, demonstrated a fearsome capacity, especially in that last great German offensive that was to produce Haig's Special Order of the Day on 11 April 1918: 'There is no course open to us but to fight it out. With our backs to the wall and believing in the justice of our cause, each one of us must fight to the end'. (The use of the initial adverbial clause in the second sentence gives the order a tingle of inspiration that normally eluded his writing.) In May, 1918, Lloyd George was faced by the fact that the onslaught might defeat the Allies before the Americans were ready to commit their forces in strength: 'Can't you see that the war will be lost unless we get this support?' he asked Pershing in exasperation. 'Gentlemen, I have thought this programme over very deliberately, and will not be co-erced,' was the chilling response. Because victory came so soon, we tend to forget how threatening the spring and summer of 1918 were. As late as 4 June Sir Maurice Hankey, the Secretary of the War Cabinet, wrote in his diary: 'I do not like the outlook. The Germans are fighting better than the Allies, and I cannot exclude the possibility of disaster'. Even in August, Haig was sufficiently downhearted to contemplate a negotiated ceasefire.

The vigour of the German attack contrasted with the stationary tactics of establishing and investing entrenched defences that had prevailed for the preceding three-and-a-half years. They achieved, for example, an advance of fourteen miles in one day in this 1918 offensive, the biggest advance in one day on the Western Front. In six weeks the Allies lost 350,000 men. Further, there was still the logistically insoluble problem of bringing artillery and supplies up to support fast-advancing infantry. But the Allies had reserves and the Americans were arriving to fill the gaps, whereas the Germans had no reserves and no *matériel* to defend their extended Front or exploit their successes, which in reality had taken them as well as their enemies by surprise.

It is worth remembering that by the end of the War 11% of France's entire population were killed or wounded as opposed to 9% of Germany's. (The non-Continental powers, Britain and America, lost respectively 8% and 0.37%.)

The officers of the New Armies were well trained for their job, because that job was not to have a technical mastery of their weapons or, as subalterns, to have a profound understanding of strategy or even tactics, but to demonstrate leadership. These young men were ideally qualified for that. Their whole background had trained them to behave as heroes, to keep upper lips stiff, to play the game. Virtually unarmed, some dribbling a football to keep their pace down, they walked ahead of their men across no-man's land, easy targets for the German snipers and machine-gunners, who were told to pick them off, leaving their men leaderless.

There has been much debate on whether there was a lost generation and if so what it consisted of. Numerically those who died in the War were about the total of those who would otherwise have gone to work in the Empire and the Dominions. Such men, it is argued, had the get-up-and-go spirit that would have made them get up and go abroad, and therefore the idea of a lost generation is an illusion. The argument is specious for several reasons. Most significantly, those who volunteered were manifestly not seeking to advance their careers, but to sacrifice themselves in the furtherance of their duty. A generation of idealists and visionaries died in no-man's-land. Many objective observers noted later the dearth of talent that the war had caused. One good observer is Alanbrooke, who recorded in his *Diaries* as Chief of the Imperial General Staff in the dark days of the Second World War the serious gaps in public life left by the earlier War.

And indeed these gaps were more serious in his profession than anywhere else. Those who led from the front as subalterns or warrant officers were so dreadfully reduced that from the 1920s onwards there was a serious shortage of talent in the British Army. This may have much to do with Churchill's impatience with his generals in the Second World War.

This, in terms of tactics and military thought, was the background in early 1916, as the 9th Battalion moved in and out of the Front Line. There were no major conflicts, but losses continued. On one day alone, for instance, in March 1916, two officers and two other ranks were killed and sixteen other ranks wounded. Again, on 29 April, the Battalion was a victim of a German gas attack. The gas had been directed against the 16th (Irish) Division who were to the south, but there was a change of wind, the gas was strong and not mixed with smoke and was therefore difficult to see. The gas blew back over the 9th after the men had removed their masks.

By July the Battalion was resting at Béthune, where between the 14th and 18th of the month Highland Games were held. On the 16th a new commanding officer, Lieutenant-Colonel S. A. Innes, assumed command and on 23 July two officers reported for duty: Second Lieutenants D. W. Cuthbert and T. E. Reid. The metamorphosis from civilian to warrior had been completed.

In a letter to Tom after Ernest's death, Colonel Innes described Cuthbert as Ernest's best friend in the Battalion. As well as reporting to the 9th Battalion on the same day, they were, in tragic synchronicity, to be fatally wounded on the same day.

By this time the Battle on the Somme was well under way. There were rumours of a move to the Battle, and it was soon announced that after relief by the 2nd Battalion Lincolnshire Regiment on 22 July, the 9th would move to Houchin and then march south to the River Somme.

It is interesting to speculate about the sort of welcome which Ernest and his friend received in the Battalion mess. Some messes were extraordinarily unfriendly to subalterns. Robert Graves, who

was commissioned in the Royal Welch Fusiliers, was initially posted
to the Welsh Regiment (different regiment, different spelling), and
he described his reception when he eventually reached the mess of
his own Regiment. He had already commanded a company, but as a
mere lieutenant he was quite ignored, as was one lieutenant who had
no less than six years' service. Only officers of the rank of captain
were allowed to drink whisky or turn on the gramophone. Shorts
were worn, because the Battalion chose to regard itself as still being
in India. French civilians were treated as natives in the sub-continent would have been and army Hindustani was talked at them.
Subalterns were referred to as 'warts'. When Graves went into the
mess he said, as was customary when a new officer entered a mess:

'Good morning, gentlemen.' There was no reply. We filed into
the room in which the mess dined, a ball-room with mirrors
and a decorated ceiling, and took our places at a long, polished
table. The seniors sat at the top, the juniors competed for seats
as far away from them as possible. Unluckily I got a seat at the
foot of the table, facing the colonel, the adjutant, and Buzz Off
[the Second-in-Command]. Not a word was spoken down my
end, except an occasional whisper for the salt or the beer –
very thin French stuff. Robertson, who had not been warned,
asked the mess-waiter for whisky. 'Sorry, sir,' said the mess-
waiter, 'it's against orders for the young officers.' Robertson
was a man of forty-two, a solicitor with a large practice, and
had stood for Parliament in the Yarmouth division at the
previous election.

I saw Buzz Off glaring at us and busied myself with my
meat and potatoes. He nudged the adjutant, 'Who are those
two funny ones down there, Charley?' he asked.

'New this morning from the militia. Answer to the names
of Robertson and Graves.'

'Which is which?' asked the colonel,

'I'm Robertson, sir.'

'I wasn't asking you.'

Robertson winced but said nothing. Then Buzz Off noticed something.

'T'other wart's wearing a wind-up tunic.' Then he bent forward and asked me loudly: 'You there, wart! Why the hell are you wearing your stars on your shoulder instead of your sleeve?'

My mouth was full, and everybody had his eyes on me. I swallowed the lump of meat whole and said: 'Shoulder stars were a regimental order in the Welsh Regiment, sir. I understood that it was the same everywhere in France.'

The colonel turned puzzled to the adjutant: 'Why on earth is the man talking about the Welsh Regiment?' And then to me: 'As soon as you have finished your lunch you will visit the master-tailor. Report at the orderly room when you're properly dressed.'

This may have been extreme, but it was not completely atypical of what happened to volunteer officers in France, who were often joining regulars who had never expected to see more than a few light skirmishes in India. The social composition of the Black Watch varied between its different battalions. The messes of the Territorial battalions were largely composed of professional people and Perthshire bourgeoisie, but the Regular battalions were much more socially rarefied. The Black Watch was the senior Highland Regiment, and although the days of buying and selling commissions were past, in 1914 – and indeed until the 1930s – there was still a very real officer class. An officer's pay was not enough to cover his mess bills and a private income was required. I cannot believe, all the same, that a Scottish mess could ever be as impossible as the Welsh one that Graves described. The 3rd Battalion must have been democratised by the flow of people of all backgrounds who came through its hands, and the 9th, as a Service Battalion, would be reasonably free of the encrusted snobbery as well as the history of an older unit. In any event, it is difficult to think that the sort of behaviour that Graves described could have survived life on the Western Front: the Royal Welch Fusiliers had been lucky: as part of the 19th Brigade, it had been practically undamaged by the early part of the war.

Ernest's first experience of life with his new Battalion was the move to the south which began on 23 July with a march of 14 miles. On 26 July, with the Division it began a much longer march of 64 miles, which was completed in six stages. There were problems. A large number of men fell out because of bad feet and difficulty with the exercise after a long spell in the trenches. Heavily loaded transport wagons had difficulty also. It was about two days before the Division was in good form. Typically robustly, and with precise arithmetic, Buchan and Stewart in the Divisional history assert that 'the fighting value of the Division was increased fifty per cent by this march to the south'.

The 9th initially found itself in reserve south of Martinpuich, in very different conditions from those in the Loos salient. Instead of living in the trenches, everyone was in the open and appeared unconcerned by even more shelling than they had formerly experienced. In tents, the men found themselves with nothing but canvas between them and the shrapnel, but further on they were in dugouts which had been taken over from the Germans. The Battalion was astonished to find that for two years the enemy had lived in comfort in their very front line. The German commander at Fricourt, for example, had a dug-out consisting of several rooms, furnished with beds, kitchen and so forth and he had not only his wife and daughter installed with him, but even his daughter's governess.

Why was the Battalion on the Somme? Everyone knows something of the Battle of the Somme. The barrage that preceded it was the biggest there had ever been. One hundred thousand shells a day were fired. When the wind was in the right direction the noise could be heard in London, 150 miles away. On the first day alone of the battle, 1 July 1916, 58,000 British troops were lost, a third of them killed. Sixty per cent of all the officers were killed on that first day, which remains a record in the awful annals of war. Typically and provocatively, Alan Taylor said, 'The Somme had [by July 1916] no longer any purpose as a field of battle. No strategical prize would be gained even if there were a great advance. The Somme had been chosen in December 1915 solely because British and French could fight here side by side. Now the French had few divisions to spare . . . moreover the Somme was peculiarly unsuited as an object of attack. The Germans everywhere occupied the crests of the hills; the attackers had to fight their way upwards against a concealed enemy'.

In reality, the reason that France contributed less than planned to the Somme attack reflected one of the main reasons it was thought to be necessary. At the start of 1916 the German Chief of Staff, von Falkenhayn, promised to 'bleed France white', and because of the onslaught on Verdun the French demanded that the attack on the Somme, which had been planned for 1 August, be brought forward to 1 July. This was agreed. In the interim, the Brusilov offensive pulled German troops to the eastern front and took some of the pressure off Verdun. With hindsight, then, it can be seen that the British attack on the Somme was not justified by Verdun, where German pressure was lessening. The most powerful reason for the Somme, however, may well have lain simply in Haig's unshakeable belief that the war could be won here. It soon became clear to most observers that this was not the case. The barrage was less effective than had been expected. There were many dud shells. The German defences were reasonably sound against the bombardment, and no-man's-land was so cut up that it was difficult for the British to advance. At home, Sir William Robertson, Chief of the Imperial General Staff, wrote to Haig on 29 July 1916: 'The powers that be are beginning to get a little uneasy in regard to the situation'. They doubted 'whether a loss of say 300,000 men will lead to really great results, because, if not, we ought to be content with something less than we are doing now . . . It is thought that the primary object – relief of pressure on Verdun – has to some extent been achieved'. Haig replied with customary assurance, 'In another six weeks, the enemy should be hard put to find men. The maintenance of a steady offensive pressure will result eventually in his complete overthrow'.

With his cavalry ready for the mounted breakthrough he confidently expected, Haig refused to be disheartened. He continued to order further attacks, each of which he expected to break the enemy. Sir Philip Gibbs later described what he had seen in July 1916 and reflected on Haig's dream of a cavalry advance:

Before dawn, in the darkness, I stood with a mass of cavalry opposite Fricourt. Haig as a cavalry man was obsessed with the idea that he would break the German line and send the cavalry through. It was a fantastic hope, ridiculed by the German High Command in their report on the Battles of the Somme which afterwards we captured.

In front of us was not a line but a fortress position, twenty miles deep, entrenched and fortified, defended by masses of machine-gun posts and thousands of guns in a wide arc. No chance for cavalry! But on that night they were massed behind the infantry. Among them were the Indian cavalry, whose dark faces were illuminated now and then for a moment, when someone struck a match to light a cigarette.

Before dawn there was a great silence. We spoke to each other in whispers, if we spoke. Then suddenly our guns opened out in a barrage of fire of colossal intensity. Never before, and I think never since, even in the Second World War, had so many guns been massed behind any battle front. It was a rolling thunder of shell fire, and the earth vomited flame, and the sky was alight with bursting shells. It seemed as though nothing could live, not an ant, under that stupendous artillery storm. But Germans in their deep dugouts lived, and when our waves of men went over they were met by deadly machine-gun and mortar fire.

Our men got nowhere on the first day. They had been mown down like grass by German machine-gunners who, after our barrage had lifted, rushed out to meet our men in the open. Many of the best Battalions were almost annihilated, and our casualties were terrible.

General Rees, who commanded the 94th Infantry Brigade at the Somme:

They advanced in line after line, dressed as if on parade, and not a man shirked going through the extremely heavy barrage, or facing the machine-gun and rifle fire that finally wiped them out. I saw the lines which advanced in such admirable order melting away under the fire. Yet not a man wavered, broke the ranks, or attempted to come back. I have never seen, I would never have imagined, such a magnificent display of gallantry, discipline and determination. The reports I have had from the very few survivors of this marvellous advance bear out what I saw with my own eyes, viz, that hardly a man of ours got to the German front line.

A German machine-gunner described the phenomenon from his perspective:

The officers were in the front. I noticed one of them walking calmly carrying a walking stick. When we started firing we just had to load and reload. They went down in their hundreds. You didn't have to aim, we just fired into them.

Even John Buchan, normally a bloodthirsty commentator, was moved by what he saw, though he was more interested in using the experience for literary effect than to draw lessons from it:

The British moved forward in line after line, dressed as if on parade; not a man wavered or broke ranks; but minute by minute the ordered lines melted away under the deluge of high explosives, shrapnel, rifle, and machine-gun fire. The splendid troops shed their blood like water for the liberty of the world.

The battle did not finally end till 18 November, when the allies had won an area approximately twelve miles long by six miles wide. Each side had sustained more than half a million casualties. In his *War Memoirs*, Lloyd George reflected:

> It is claimed that the Battle of the Somme destroyed the old German Army by killing off its best officers and men. It killed off far more of our best and of the French best. The Battle of the Somme was fought by the volunteer armies raised in 1914 and 1915. These contained the choicest and best of our young manhood. The officers came mainly from our public schools and universities. Over 400,000 of our men fell in this bull-headed fight and the slaughter amongst our young officers was appalling.

He points out that even the *Official History of the War* said:

> For the disastrous loss of the finest manhood of the United Kingdom and Ireland there was only a small gain of ground to show . . . Munitions and the technique of their use improved, but never again was the spirit or the quality of the officers and men so high, nor the general state of the training, leading and above all, discipline of the new British armies in France so good. The losses sustained were not only heavy but irreplaceable.

This was the tragic battle in which the 9th Battalion was to take part. It arrived at the Front fortunately after the appalling opening day was past. The fighting in which it was to take part was described officially as 'the opening of the wearing-out Battle'. The Battalion history says, astonishingly, 'Beginning on July 1st with a Franco-British attack on the 25 mile front astride the Somme, the first two phases of the battle had already been reasonably successful'. The third phase was to consist in a series of engagements for the possession of the plateau facing the allies, a plateau about 500 feet in height, which dominated the country to the north-east and south-west.

The detailed history of the Battalion's rôle is difficult to construct, as little material is available other than the laconic reporting in the War Diary.

There was heavy fighting, in which ground was sometimes won and lost again. The trenches were in very bad condition after the shelling of the earlier stages of the battle and the ground in front was equally bad and sometimes impassable as innumerable shell holes filled up with rain water. There was scarcely a square foot of earth that had not been broken up by shell fire.

On 17 August 1916 two companies of the 9th Black Watch were sent forward to attempt to recapture a feature known as 'The Elbow' in conjunction with the Camerons. The attack was completed successfully, although during the following night consolidation work had to be suspended because of heavy enemy fire. The Black Watch companies captured one machine-gun and seven men, but the losses were severe: one officer was killed and six were wounded, along with 25 other ranks killed, 113 wounded and 12 missing, a total of 157. The Battalion medical officer, Captain F. A. Bearn, whom we have met already at Loos assisted by Emilienne Moreau and her pistol, was severely wounded and left the unit. He had received the Military Cross for his services at Loos, and later was awarded the DSO for subsequent work. He was known in the Battalion as 'The Apothecary'. While in the rat-infested trenches near Loos, he was in the habit of using the rodents for target practice with his revolver. One evening, seeing a rat sitting in the dark, he took aim and fired. The animal did not move. He took another shot at it. It still failed to budge and it was only when he went forward to look at it that he found he had been firing at a live Mills grenade.

After further service on the line, there was a short period in reserve. In September the Battalion was in the Front Line again. Initially preparatory work had to be done to the trenches, creating 'jumping off' trenches, fire-steps and saps. All of this was done under continuous shell- and machine-gun fire, as the Battalion occupied a position overlooked by the Germans in what was called High Wood. On 7 September the Battalion was ordered to attack an enemy trench, just outside the north-west corner of High Wood, the following day. The rôle that Ernest had been playing in the Battalion until now is not known in detail. He would be a platoon commander and as well as commanding his platoon in any major offensives would be involved in leading patrols or raids or minor skirmishes. But we do know more about his rôle in this operation, when he was under the command of Captain Binnie, who was awarded the Military Cross following the attack. Ernest received a minor wound, a slight scratch on the face. If minor injuries of that sort are taken into account, then in that particular raid only two of the 20 officers involved were not either killed, wounded or missing. Captain Binnie himself received a minor wound which was not significant enough to be recorded in the Battalion history. The attack was carried out by 'B' & 'D' Companies under the command of Captains Stirling and Binnie. Ernest was part of 'D' Company. The operation began at 6.30 p.m. and despite heavy machine-gun fire the enemy trench was taken and 30 prisoners were captured. The Black Watch immediately attempted to consolidate their position and were able to repel a strong enemy counter-attack made an hour later. They had been supported by a battalion on the right which found that it could not maintain its position and announced that it was retiring. There was then pressure from the Germans on that flank as well as on the front and also some opposition on the left flank. By 8.00 p.m. 'B' & 'D' Companies had to fall back to the original Front Line, sustaining some losses as they did so.

As well as the casualties among the officers, 24 other ranks were killed, 14 missing and 59 seriously wounded. Against that, in addition to prisoners taken, 70 Germans were killed.

After the usual period of rest, the Battalion moved again to the Front Line in the Martinpuich sector on 17 September. There they had a particularly unpleasant time. They were deluged not only by heavy artillery fire, but also by torrents of rain which turned the half-finished trenches into a quagmire. In the bare two days they spent there they lost seven other ranks, 37 wounded and one missing. In the period from 12 August to 19 September they had lost 63 officers and other ranks with 30 missing and 304 wounded, in addition to which six officers and 71 other ranks had been evacuated sick.

After one final tour again only lasting two days, the Battalion spent the rest of their time in the Somme area in conditions which the Battalion history describes as 'peaceful as far as actual fighting was concerned'. Not too much should be read into these reassuring words: the history goes on to say that there was continuous heavy shelling by day and night which inflicted casualties; and even worse was the condition of the areas in which the men lived, exacerbated by the weather. Until the Division had constructed them themselves, there were few dug-outs. The only shelters were narrow slits in the ground, and most of the 'trenches' were no more than chains of waterlogged shell holes. Rations had to be carried up four miles by men from the Reserve Company. Frequently soldiers had to be dug out of the mud into which they had fallen and which threatened to drown them.

It would be in these conditions that Ernest wrote the two letters to Ronald which have survived. On 28 October 1916 he thanked Ronald for a letter he had received. He had been thinking of applying for a transfer to the Royal Flying Corps, but said that he did not intend to make an application until he had leave. Note that after seeing action on the Somme, Ernest was now preparing to transfer to the Royal Flying Corps, the only place in the war where the casualty rate was higher than it was for subalterns on the Western Front. He was not expecting leave soon, but:

[t]hey might start allowing two or perhaps three officers away each week in which case my turn wouldn't be so very long in coming.

I see quite a lot of harmless huns occasionally on a road a few miles away. They work at keeping the road in order, though to tell you the truth, they don't work much at all. They belong to what you might call the 'leasured classes.' [A family joke, referring to the pronunciation of political demagogues of the time.] I suppose the idea of giving them an easy time is to encourage more to join the happy band. The bosches [sic] often come over and surrender because they are fed up with the war. I was hearing today of an officer [German] who told his men not to fire on our troops when they were attacking so that he and his men would get taken prisoner and be finished with the war.

I was reading in Punch that very probably the Kaiser would be very much pleased to have command of a steam-roller on the road. The old huns work the steamrollers and everything.

He ended by referring to the hens with which the family at Hazelwood was attempting to supplement its wartime diet:

You must have made a bit of a change in the henhouse. Is the roof sloping? If it isn't, the rain will be apt to come in.

It must have required an effort to throw himself into the effects of rain on the hens when he himself was deep in mud. The conditions were in fact so bad that General McCracken decided that battalions would spend only two days in the Front Line at one time. Although the measure was well meant, the result was that miles had to be walked through churned-up and waterlogged country, discounting the effect of longer 'rest' periods. The conditions resulted in a high level of sickness, and even when battalions were in Divisional Reserve under canvas (in December), they were wading through eight inches or more of mud, without flooring boards in the tents.

Ernest wrote again to Ronald on 7 December, again in response to a letter from Ronald, which appears to have been something of a rarity:

I am glad to hear that you are quite better now [Ronald suffered from asthma and was very frequently ill as a child]. Be sure and stick in at school. Remember that it is a poor chap who is neither good at work nor at play. So if you can't manage to shine at your lessons [never, in fact, a problem for Ronald, who perversely enjoyed examinations], do your best at football. A big hefty chap like you should be able to become very good with plenty of practice. And as you practise and improve you will get to like it more and more. So much for my little sermon.

Thanks so much for your letter which came yesterday. It interested me immensely. I hope you will write oftener in future.

He then returned to the hens:

I suppose you won't be getting many eggs from the hens just now. The Exchequer Leghorns should be beginning to lay very early, perhaps next month. I believe they have been known to start laying when they were four months old.

He deals with one or two Paisley friends:

You tell me that Margaret Watt is driving her father's car in uniform. Does that mean something striking? Breeches or something out of the way like that.

The Sergeant Major has just come back from leave. He does not think Scotland nearly such a good place as he expected it would be. He said that one can be fined for striking a match in the street at night or flashing an electric torch. And he says that a certain Co-operative Society allows [only] 2 lbs of sugar a week to each family, no matter what the size of the family.

Out here we at least get enough sugar and men smoke and consequently light matches even less than 100 yards from the Germans.

Still in spite of all the hardships at home, I'll be delighted when leave comes.

By the end of the year the Battalion were in Brigade Reserve where they heard that in the New Year's Honours List Colonel

Innes and Captain F. A. Bearn, R.A.M.C., 'the Apothecary', had received DSOs.

Before leaving for the Arras Front, the Battalion was in the Front Line twice more in January and it celebrated its New Year dinner late, on 8 January.

Ernest may have missed the New Year dinner because the leave that he had been hoping for arrived in January and this young veteran of the Somme returned home to his family for two precious weeks.

At the end of that leave, there occurred a particularly moving little cameo. Presumably wanting to avoid an emotional farewell with his parents, Ernest went with just Ronald on the short walk to Paisley West Station. Railway stations seem particularly associated with wartime partings in the twentieth century. Ernest asked Ronald, no doubt to flatter the 13-year-old, to carry his officer's cane for him. When they got to the station he gave him a tip. I do not remember whether it was half-a-crown (two shillings and sixpence, 12.5p), or five shillings (25p). The former would be worth about £12.50 today and the latter £25, and either was far more than carrying a swagger stick for a quarter of a mile was worth and far more than Ernest could afford to give. Ronald never forgave himself for accepting the tip and never had a chance to give it back, because Ernest was leaving Scotland for the last time.

9

The Meeting-Point of Two Highways

ARRAS

The difference between 1916 and 1917 was the difference between idealism and disillusionment. The heady patriotism of 1914, the mood of the Happy Warrior, did not last long, but it was replaced, for a time, at least, by a confident belief (at least on the part of those who were not at the heart of the direction of affairs, political or military) that the war could be brought to an end by the arrival of Kitchener's New Armies, supported by enormous artillery onslaughts on the German lines. These hopes were to die on the Somme, along arguably with much of Britain's national confidence and the beliefs that had inspired Victorian and Edwardian society. After the Somme, plans were of course laid for subsequent offensives, but one senses that the General Staff went about their work more because that was what they were there for than because they felt they had found the secret of victory. When the war did end, it was more the result of exhaustion and collapse on the part of the losers than of the strategic vision of the victors.

Civilian morale frequently failed to correspond to military events, a disengagement which infantry officers on leave such as Sassoon found difficult to accept; but even from the civilian perspective there can have been little to raise the spirits of Tom and Annie as they entered 1917. Ernest had told them the grim statistics of life and death on the Western Front and revealed the scant chances of his survival. This surprised Ronald in retrospect, though he concluded that Ernest wanted them to be prepared for what might happen. If they looked at the map they would see that the line of the trenches had altered little in the two years since the fluidity of the first months of the war. All that had happened was that the trenches were much stronger and better reinforced. Consolidation of the trenches by considerable engineering work was particularly marked on the German side. If a breakthrough had proved impossible when the trenches were in the early stages of their evolution, the chance of movement now seemed correspondingly less likely.

In January 1917 the prospect of American involvement in the war seemed remote. Anyway, the American army numbered only a little over 100,000 men: it was the seventeenth army in the world in terms of size. War was to be declared on Germany by the United States on 6 April 1917, but it was a long time before conscription and adaptation to a war economy would make the American contribution significant in material terms; and there was every possibility that the Allies could be defeated in the meantime, as Ludendorff's offensive in the spring of 1918 was to show.

The German U-boat campaign was affecting the feeding of the civilian population by early 1917, although the situation did not become seriously worrying for another six months. The Reids in Hazelwood were in any event able to supplement their diet. Annie had enormous confidence in Lloyd George (she would have been amazed had she known that he was referred to by those who knew him best as 'The Goat'), and when he said that gardens should be turned over to the production of food, the lawns were dug up and planted with vegetables. The Exchequer Leghorns added protein to the diet.

Above all, inexorably continuing casualties eroded the morale of those at home, especially those with loved ones at the Front – and few families were not in this position. The *Glasgow Herald* that arrived at Hazelwood every day, like all the other national newspapers printed on its front page that day's Roll of Honour. Friends and acquaintances, if not relatives, would appear all too often, and in many households the reading of the paper was banned until after breakfast so that tragedy could be held at bay for at least another hour.

Militarily, things were even more dispiriting. On all sides the Armies were by now fragile: 1917 was, in the words of Sir John Keegan, the year of 'the breaking of armies'. The French army was at Verdun, defending, almost as a sacred duty, a salient on their own soil where 216,337 men were ultimately to be wounded, 61,289 killed and 10,151 classified as 'missing': mutilated beyond identification or no longer recognisable as human bodies. Before the year was out, much of French martial resolve was to disintegrate into what were effectively withdrawals of labour, strikes by the soldiers. As early as February 1917 General Nivelle had reported what he regarded as a dangerous climate, essentially of a political character. He considered that revolutionaries, anarchists and syndicalists were attempting to promote strikes and sabotage. Early in May, two regiments that had suffered badly on the first day of Nivelle's offensive refused to return to the Front. Their attitude was an ambivalent amalgam of slogans such as 'Down with the War! Death to those who are responsible!', compounded by comparison of their pay with what munitions workers were earning. The mutiny spread through the 4th, 5th, 6th and 10th Armies, the units that had taken most punishment in Nivelle's offensive. Civilians struck in sympathy. In reality, the French soldiers, who had displayed immense courage under fire, were not mutineering, so much as trying to make a considered statement to the effect that current strategy was a failure; and part of Pétain's adept handling of the situation was to combine sympathetic treatment of the ordinary soldiers with a shift in tactics and a substitution of limited objectives for grandiose schemes. But punishment was meted out too: the special military tribunals he set up found 3,427 men guilty of mutinous offences. Between 500 and 600 men were sentenced to death, around 75 shot and some 100 exiled to the colonies.

Russia's war effort collapsed, the Revolution took place and by October Russia was no longer a combatant. Italy's army broke after the defeat at Caporetto in October. British military morale, badly eroded by the Somme in 1916, was to suffer grievously in the mud of the Third Battle of Ypres/Passchendaele in October 1917. The German army had exhausted its resources of manpower by the end of 1917. While the same was essentially true of Britain and France, they had far greater material resources and they could look to America for reinforcements in personnel.

This was the framework within which the Battle of Arras took place. 'Battles' were the names given in the First World War to the campaigns that made up the war as a whole. Their definition is arbitrary and they are used to encompass operations planned for particular Fronts at particular times. Technically, the Battle of Arras consists of the Battle of Vimy, the first Battle of the Scarpe, the second Battle of the Scarpe, the attack on La Coulotte, the Battle of Arleux, the third Battle of the Scarpe, the capture of Roeux and the capture of Oppy Ridge. There were also four flanking battles on the Bullecourt Flank and three flanking battles on the Lens Flank. The engagement in which Ernest was wounded is known as the Capture of Monchy, which forms part of the first Battle of the Scarpe.

Sometimes these offensives, such as the Somme, were planned in a spirit of strategic optimism, and some, such as the German offensive in March 1918, in a spirit of grim necessity. Frequently, however, they seem to have been planned to assuage public opinion at home, to relieve pressure on an ally or simply for the sake of something to do. The Easter offensive of 1917, of which the Battle of Arras was the British component, had first been envisaged at the Chantilly Conference in November 1916. Offensives were planned on various Fronts, with the main effort to be on the Somme battle-field. Shortly after the Conference, however, France substituted Nivelle for Joffre as Commander-in-Chief. Nivelle amended Joffre's plan and, as an artillery man, chose to ignore the Somme battlefield, scarred and broken as it was by the warfare of the previous year. He preferred to bring a huge artillery barrage to bear on the German Front on either side of the Somme salient, delivered by the French on the south sector in the region of the Aisne and by the British at the northern end, at Vimy Ridge and Arras. The rich, flat lands of Northern France, Germany and Flanders faced the Allies, rich with a soil that is fecund both in agricultural and mineral terms.

Before the offensive opened, the Germans in fact negated Joffre's original purpose by withdrawing along the Somme Front to the Hindenburg Line, which shortened their exposure and established them in a more heavily fortified position. The line did not extend as far as the projected French attack to the south or as far as the British attack to the north.

Arras is bypassed today by the autoroute A26 which runs more or less on top of the Hindenburg Line and its southern extension, the Drocourt-Quéant Switch Line, or Wotan Stellung, which was created in place of the former salient at Gommecourt. The old Route Nationale running from Arras to Cambrai is roughly where the British Line was. With much of the traffic taken away by the autoroute, the Nationale, running dead straight between these two killing fields, carries little traffic, and as one drives along it one senses an air of sombre stillness.

Nivelle came to Arras having demonstrated great ability at Verdun in co-ordinating artillery and infantry. 'Laon in twenty-four hours,' he assured Paris, 'and then we break out.' His strategy would result in what he called 'rupture' of the German lines; the artillery barrage would allow his forces to move straight through to open ground to the rear of the German lines, leaving behind them only pockets of surviving German troops. There was here the hope for a more open warfare than the Western Front had seen since 1914. He informed his government that he could end the war in two days. London, and in particular Lloyd George, found him no less persuasive: his mother was English, and he spoke her language fluently – and with a reassuringly upper-class accent. But apart from flaws in his strategy, his plans leaked extensively and as a result the German line opposite his front on the Aisne was particularly well built up in anticipation of the offensive. His fluency in English contributed to the failure of his offensive as he notoriously discussed his plans at dinners in London in front of society ladies who were not reliably reticent about what they heard.

Controversy continues to surround the reputation of Douglas Haig. On the one hand there is the picture - it is even to be found in GCSE core material – of 'the butcher of the Somme', an image so widely accepted that there has been a move to have his statue removed from Whitehall. On the other hand there is a body of scholars who seek to rehabilitate him and his role in the transformation of the army into an efficient, modern fighting force through what is called the 'learning curve'. Haig's supporters are much more informed than his detractors, but both sides express themselves with equal intemperance.

There *was* a transformation in the army. In 1914 artillery techniques were primitive and the infantry were essentially riflemen, fighting rather as they had done in the eighteenth century. Indeed trench warfare owed much to the science of war in the sixteenth and seventeenth centuries, when the same citadels and castles in Flanders had been invested in much the same way. Well before 1918 all that had changed. Infantry tactics in particular had undergone a complete transformation. There was far less reliance on the rifle: infantry was part of an all-arms cooperation, and its armoury included mortars, Lewis guns, machine-guns, trench mortars, hand grenades and rifle grenades. War was being fought as it would be until the mechanisation of the 1970s. Haig did not just preside over all this; he pushed for the change, pressing for more tanks, seeing the possibilities of aircraft, encouraging the intelligent use of terrain. Finally, in 'the Hundred Days', he led his armies, when France was exhausted and demoralised, in the great series of unchecked, British-led victories that brought the war to an end.

He was not a military visionary, no Marlborough or Wellington. But he was a good general, an efficient general, and quite certainly the best available to Britain during the First World

War. And that is the point. The British high command cannot have been exclusively composed of dunderheads, and he was the best of it. Churchill, critical of the direction of the war on the Western Front, conceded that; and even Lloyd George, bitterly antagonistic to Haig, and who had the army searched for a possible replacement, admitted that he could not find one.

None of which means that Haig was a sympathetic character. He was a private, unimaginative man, with little sense of humour, vain and solipsistic. On the eve of Third Ypres/Passchendaele he could find time to write to his wife about a post-war biography. He cavilled about the level of peerage he was to receive at the end of the war – and even about his position in the Victory Parade.

His appointment as Commander-in-Chief had not been secured without some manoeuvring, and he took steps to consolidate his position. He wrote up his diary on a duplicate pad, and a King's Messenger took a copy back every night to his wife (on one occasion along with some soup prepared by Haig's chef for a convalescing Lady Haig). She was encouraged to show the copies to the King for personal propaganda purposes. After the war the diary was rewritten where necessary to improve on the historical record.

He regretted the blood-letting, and he was later to work hard for ex-service men, but unlike say his predecessor, Sir John French, he was able to detach himself professionally from the carnage. Churchill compared him to an early surgeon, the kindest of men outside the operating theatre, but in it recognising that blood would be lost, and that if the patient died, that was something that just had to be accepted.

He had spent his whole life doggedly making himself fit for command, and his strong views were not refined by self-doubt. He was perfectly clear that Britain was fighting a just war, not for selfish reasons, but for the benefit of humanity. He was probably not the most interesting person to sit beside at dinner, but it was as well that he was available for his country's service when he was.

His relations with his Army Commanders were distant. At

General Headquarters the Commanders were known as 'The Wicked Barons' (scarcely a band of brothers), and he tended to leave them alone to deal with tactics (although he could interfere in 'grand tactics'), while he concerned himself with issues of strategy.

Haig's Army Commander at the Battle of Arras was Edmund Allenby, who commanded Third Army, of which 15th (Scottish) Division was part. A tense relationship had existed for some time between Haig and Allenby, both cavalrymen, which may have originated in their first acquaintance with each other, at Staff College, Camberley, when Allenby was elected Master of the Drag Hounds in preference to the reserved and prickly Haig.

Haig may have been on the defensive as he had been *sent* to Camberley, whereas Allenby and most of the others had won their way there by competitive examination. Allenby was reputed to be clever, whereas Haig's strength was said to be in application. There was certainly an undercurrent of rivalry. It was not expressed in any disloyalty on Allenby's part. He did not intrigue against Haig, and would tolerate no criticism of G.H.Q. amongst his officers. Both were meticulously polite in their contacts with each other, although at weekly meetings with the Army Commanders, Haig was inclined to interrupt Allenby's contributions.

Communications between the two cannot have been easy in any case, as they were both outstandingly reticent, even inarticulate. Haig conversed by grunts and half-finished sentences, and his silences at lunch and dinner at G.H.Q. were notorious. One aide described him struggling with such commonplace utterances as 'Thank you very much. Good', which he described as, coming from Haig, a major speech. Allenby was only slightly better. But though a man of few words, they were so forcefully expressed that he was widely known as 'the Bull'. He made his views equally clear to his superiors and his subordinates and his popularity suffered accordingly. He was in fact solicitous for the welfare of his men, but they were less conscious of that than of his outbursts when, on visits to forward units, he came across any breaches of regulations.

Only one officer, Sir John Keir, of VI Corps, regularly stood up to the Bull: inevitably he became known as 'the Toreador'.

At the very beginning of the Battle of Arras, any difficulty in relations between Haig and Allenby was exacerbated when the Commander-in-Chief interfered in what he regarded as grand tactics. Allenby wanted to give the Germans as little warning of the offensive as possible, limiting shelling to a hurricane bombardment of 48 hours, with breaks only to allow the barrels to cool down and the men to eat. Haig, on the other hand, wanted a more conventional bombardment, lasting five days. What Allenby desired may not have been technically feasible and Haig was generally supported in his view, but the tactics by which he ensured that his view would prevail were interesting. Allenby's artillery expert, Major-General Holland, supported him and had in fact been responsible for recommending the two-day bombardment. At G.H.Q., Haig's artillery adviser, Major-General Birch, took the other view, and he turned Allenby's flank by having Holland promoted to command a corps.

Those were the plans that brought Ernest to Arras in April 1917. Before looking at how they were to affect him and his family at home in Hazelwood, it is worth looking briefly at how they affected the outcome of the war.

The British attack began on 9 April 1917, the French a week later. A huge artillery bombardment took place, employing 2,800 guns for five days. The period of the bombardment was shorter than on the Somme, but the number of shells delivered on to the German defences was twice as many. The Canadians, north of Arras, took Vimy Ridge, an important geographical feature, after three hours of heavy fighting. Near Arras itself, the Third Army advanced three and a half miles. This was the biggest gain since the trenches had been dug in 1914. To the south of the River Scarpe, where the 9th Battalion fought, the advance was much less. Significantly, the Germans were able to hold the village strongpoint of Monchy-le-Preux, which was to be Ernest's objective, against repeated British attacks.

Looking at the picture as a whole, at the end of the first day the success of the British and Canadians appeared remarkable. Captain Cyril Falls, one of the official historians, described the Easter Monday attack as 'One of the great days of the War . . . among the heaviest blows struck by British arms in the Western theatre of war'. In the course of the day, Third Army took 5,600 prisoners, and the Canadians a further 3,400. Ground had been taken with relatively few casualties and the way seemed open for further advance. But the weather was appalling. The advance had begun in sleet, and rain and snow succeeded. The terrain was chalk which had been rendered into mud. Additionally, a planned pause of two hours checked the advance. Some further advances were made in the north on 12 April. Thereafter little happened until 16 April, when the French Aisne offensive began. That offensive was disastrous, the French equivalent of the Somme. On the first day alone the French suffered 40,000 casualties. Nivelle continued to attack until 20 April, before finally abandoning the offensive on 9 May. France had suffered 187,000 casualties compared to a German total of 168,000. Nivelle was swiftly removed and on 25 April replaced by Pétain. Almost immediately 'the mutinies of 1917' began.

Part of the problem was simply that there was an inability to translate the gains that had been made into movement and manoeuvre. The allied armies at this stage had no experience or knowledge of how to exploit successful punches at the German line. A limited breakthrough had been achieved but there was no forward momentum.

Haig urged Allenby, held up at Monchy, to push forward on the north of the Scarpe and then move south-east behind Monchy, so as to turn the German flank. Haig appears to have found it impossible to get divisional commanders to go forward and take control of operations. At any rate, that is the impression that he gave when on 12 April he concluded that the opportunity had been lost: 'I pointed out that the enemy had now been given time to put the Drocourt-Quéant line into a state of defence'.

In fact, it is not obvious that Allenby needed urging from Haig. Immediately after the 9 April advance, Allenby ordered his Army to continue the advance. On 10 April Haig met Allenby at St Pol and told him to continue forward where he could. On the following day, although things were by now not going well, Allenby was still optimistic – unrealistically so – and his order for the day was full of adrenalin:

> The Army commander wishes all troops to understand that Third Army is pursuing a defeated enemy and that risks must be taken.

As late as 14 April Allenby still wanted to push on, but there was a remarkable 'mutiny' by three of his divisional commanders, who criticised him and formally represented to General Headquarters that Allenby's attempts at narrow advances left vulnerably exposed flanks. Haig upheld their appeal and ordered a suspension of operations.

The factor which must have frustrated General Headquarters was that the British contribution to the Aisne offensive was essentially a subordinate one, intended to take pressure off the French operations to the north-west. In the event the British/ Canadian operations demonstrated more potential for success, if not a success which could be translated into victory.

Haig had cavalry ready at Arras, as elsewhere; they were ordered to stand by to exploit the breakthrough, but they could not be deployed. Shrapnel, machine-guns, trenches and barbed-wire entanglements made cavalry redundant, and no other medium existed for rapid advance. In any case, the German defence had stiffened, the British could not advance guns over wet ground that had been broken up by bombardment, and 3rd Cavalry Division had to dismount and defend Monchy when eventually it was taken.

Haig renewed limited action on the British Front on 3 May in an effort to encourage the French to continue fighting, but the offensive was over by the end of May. The Germans had suffered badly at Vimy and lost the northern six miles of the Hindenburg

Line, but by the end of the offensive the British had lost 150,000 men, against over 100,000 lost by the Germans. The B.E.F. daily loss rate was 4,076 at Arras, compared with 2,963 at the Somme, 2,323 at Passchendaele/Third Ypres and 3,645 in the Hundred Days battles of 1918.

Allenby did not long survive the Battle of Arras: by June he had been, in the jargon of the times, 'degummed', and relieved of his command of Third Army. The records are a trifle opaque, referring to his dismissal as being because of his conduct in command of Third Army 'and many other reasons'. It is not clear what these 'other reasons' were. He was far from happy to be dismissed, and when making a courtesy call on his successor, General Byng, 'broke down very badly'. He was being sent to Palestine, at that stage regarded as distinctly a sideshow compared to the Western Front. As things turned out, that was far from the case, and he went on to achieve a distinction in Palestine which had eluded him in France, his victory at the Battle of Megiddo, in particular, being regarded as a masterpiece.

The opening stages of the Battle of Arras had been reported in the usual style in the British newspapers. Writing in the *Daily Mail* of 10 April 1917, William Beach Thomas reported:

> Near Arras our troops leapt to the attack in the midst of such artillery fire as the world has never seen . . . [I]t is too early to give more than partial news, but the famous divisions directly in front of me . . . went straight through to their goal.

On the same day, *The Times* reported that

> The Battle of Arras, if that is what it is to be called, may prove no less than disastrous to the Germans. Such a battle as has begun this morning cannot be fought without heavy casualties. We must be reconciled to that in advance. But the enemy will suffer more than we, and we shall break him here as we broke him on the Somme.

10

Death, Becoming Death, is Dearer Far When Duty Bids you Bleed in Open War

RAILWAY TRIANGLE

That was the backdrop to the last act of Ernest's life. As he made his way forward on the path of duty that led from Paisley to Arras, he knew less about the plans made at Chantilly than the German General Staff. The path of duty was a hard one: on 14 February 1917 the 9th Battalion finally left Bresle in the Somme area for the Arras Front. Before it left, as part of the 15th Division, it received a farewell message from General Sir Herbert Rawlinson, commanding the Fourth Army, in which he said: 'I know no Division in which a higher standard of discipline and morale exists, nor one to which I would entrust a difficult undertaking with greater confidence'.

On 14 February the Division joined VI Corps (Lieutenant-General Haldane) in the Third Army (General Allenby) and began the march to Arras. The condition of the Battalion was poor. After the long periods in the line on the Somme and the weather and the mud, the men were in poor physical and mental condition as they faced a biting cold wind on a march which they found difficult and which was to last for four whole days. Eventually the Battalion reached Buneville on 18 February, and there it spent five days before moving on 23 February to Ambrimes.

Training now began again and instructions came from General Headquarters on reorganisation. On 8 March there was an inspection by the Commander-in-Chief, Haig, and three days later the Battalion went into the new Front area, relieving the 13th Royal Scots.

At this point the line ran north and south, about a quarter of a mile east of Arras. There were underground communication trenches from Arras itself which took advantage of the network of cellars and galleries below the town, so that it was possible to move from the crypt of the Cathedral to the Front Line without being observed, and reliefs could be carried out in broad daylight: the Battalion was surprised by how easily it could gain access to the front trenches.

There were billets for reserve troops within the town of Arras itself, in the large cellars and (no doubt empty) wine stores. Ernest himself was in a billet at the village of Duisans, a mile-and-a-half west of Arras. In this flat landscape, any tumulus that creates a defensive capacity has been fought over through the centuries and the signposts are rollcalls of a millennium of battles. No rise in the ground, however insignificant, has failed to support a fortress or to undergo a siege. Arras is no exception. The Romans established a legion here, but before that there was a community of Atrebates. It became part of Flanders and then it was taken by the Normans. It was held in turn by the English, the French, the Austrians and the Spanish. Joan of Arc was imprisoned here in 1431. In 1541 the English and the Spaniards fought the French. Between 1633 and 1707 a great citadel was built, designed by the ubiquitous Vauban. Marlborough took the city from the French in 1708 and the Germans took it from them in September 1914 before France recaptured it. The town was badly damaged by conventional attacks in 1915 as well as by aerial bombardment. In November 1916 forty German aeroplanes attacked the town. Despite all this, the British and French allies retained the small salient which was formed by Arras and which provided a launching point for the planned attack on the German Line.

At this stage it was intended that another unit was to undertake the advance from Arras and that the 9th Battalion would not be involved until an attack on 23 April. In the event, a shortage of manpower made it necessary for the 9th Battalion to take part in both advances. For the moment there was little activity except for severe shelling from time to time, and the Battalion was able to get on with its preparations. In the Blangy suburb of Arras, where the lines were only about fifteen yards apart, everything was particularly quiet, each side keeping the other under the closest observation.

The German defences which the Division faced consisted of three or four lines of trenches, seventy-five to one hundred yards apart and united by communication trenches. Behind them lay a support line, which was linked to the Hindenburg Line defences. Behind that again, there lay a strongly held reserve line.

Part of the preparations for the battle consisted in 'keeping up the aggressive spirit of the troops'. This was thought to be achieved by constant raids on the enemy trenches: one, on 8 April was regarded as being particularly successful.

In the meantime, on Monday 25 March Ernest was promoted to Acting Captain and placed in the command of 'A' Company. He had earlier been appointed Battalion Adjutant, the officer with responsibility for carrying out the Battalion's administrative work on behalf of the Colonel. That appointment terminated as he became a Company Commander. It is worth pausing to reflect that Ernest was now a veteran of the Somme, where he had suffered a minor wound, an Acting Captain, a Company Commander and until recently Battalion Adjutant, all at the age of just twenty years and three months.

The hours before going over the top have been well described in the literature of the Great War, but the grimness of the reality is difficult to comprehend. Each man knew that within the next few hours there was a very real chance that he would be dead and it was a certainty that many of his comrades would be. What many men feared more than extinction was an injury that would leave them maimed and incapacitated for the rest of their lives. What many men wished for was 'the blighty one', an injury that would be serious enough to have them invalided home and out of the War, but without lasting incapacity.

At 7 p.m. on Sunday 8 April, Easter Sunday, Ernest went into the staff billets of 'A' Company at Arras and gave orders to the

Company Sergeant Major that blankets and coats were to be rolled up in bundles of ten and sent to store in the town of Arras. He told them that the Battalion would go over the top at 5.30 a.m. on the following day. A rum issue was to take place at 10.30 p.m. and an issue of tea at 11 p.m. He said that those men who were not on fatigue duty should get whatever rest they could before 2.30 a.m., when everyone would leave billets to take up position in the jumping-off trench.

The object of the attack was to capture Vimy Ridge, Monchy-le-Preux and the high ground to the south of it, driving the Germans back to lower ground to the east. Initially the 15th Division was ambitiously given the burden of dealing with the whole of the first stages of the attack on Monchy. It became clear, however, that the enemy troops were far too well established for a single division to achieve this on its own, and the task for the 15th Division was scaled down to capturing and consolidating the Brown Line, the designation the Staff gave to the third line of the German defences, just east of Feuchy village. There were four lines in all successively facing the Division, designated Black (the old, pre-Hindenburg, German Front Line system), Blue (rising ground known as 'Observation Ridge'), Brown and Green lines, the last being through Monchy itself. When this had been taken, the 37th Division were to go through the 15th and capture Monchy-le-Preux. Monchy is about five miles from Arras and about 200 feet above the River Scarpe. The landscape in the vicinity of Arras is open and rolling, and Monchy, perched on relatively high ground, commanded excellent observation. The town has changed little since 1917. Apart from its historical interest it has little to bring visitors. There are no Michelin awards for its restaurants. There are indeed no restaurants, just a café which has the air of being closed *en permanence*, Le Grand Cerf (the name a reference to the statue that commemorates the Canadian capture of the village). But the elevated position made it important in 1917, as the number of Commonwealth War Graves Commission cemeteries around the town sadly underlines: there is Monchy itself, Happy Valley,

Windmill, Orange Trench, Tank, Guémappe and Feuchy, where the Visitors' Book in 2002 included an entry on behalf of a lady of 102 who remembered 'a brother still missed and loved'. A G.H.Q. notice of 2 January 1917 mentioned as one of its first objectives seizing 'the high ground about Monchy-le-Preux'. A Third Army Appreciation of 7 February 1917 said that 'Monchy-le-Preux should be in our hands by nightfall on the first day'. The commanding officer of the 13th Rifle Brigade stressed the importance of the objective in dramatic terms in his instructions to his men at 6.15 p.m. on Easter Sunday: 'Gentlemen, we will take Monchy or die'.

For the record, the village was not captured on the first or second day: it was finally captured on 11 April. But it was to be lost a year later and not recaptured until 26 August 1918.

Starting at midnight, as Easter Sunday moved into Easter Monday, the Battalion took up its position for the attack. The original planning was that the Front Line of advance should consist of 'C' Company on the right and 'D' Company on the left; the support line of 'B' Company; and 'A', Ernest's Company, was to follow in reserve. These plans were radically amended very soon. Each Company of 200 men or so was divided into four waves of about fifty men. Ernest was initially with the second wave. Each wave consisted of two lines of men.

The British trenches from which the troops moved off were four in number with about ten yards between each, the first only thirty or forty yards from the Germans. The trenches occupied by the Battalion occupied only 200 yards of the front.

The third and fourth waves served as Reserve and as Moppers-up, their job being to clear the German dug-outs of any German troops who were left and who might shoot the advancing Black Watch from behind after the first and second waves had passed through them.

After the frightful weather in which the Battalion had advanced towards Arras, conditions had been fine, but immediately the attack began on Easter Monday, rain started to fall, and it continued throughout the day, turning to snow, blinding in a gale of wind towards the end of the day. All the accounts mention how terrible the weather was.

At 2 a.m. orders were issued that the full 'A' Company was to parade in the trench behind Headquarters billets at once. Everyone was ready for the start at 2.30 a.m. but it was impossible to get a move made: communication trenches on the way to the firing line (or first trench) were completely blocked by troops advancing to take up positions. In Haig's Despatches he recognised that:

> A problem peculiar to the launching of a great offensive from a town arose from the difficulty of ensuring the punctual debouching of troops, and the avoidance of confusion and congestion in the stress both before the assault and during the progress of the battle. This problem was met by the most careful and complete organisation of routes, reflecting the highest credit on the staffs concerned.

Ernest had to dash around to sort matters out, but eventually a move was made and the Company moved off with the Company Headquarters Staff in the rear consisting of the Sergeant Major, the Company Clerk, Sergeant Dow in charge of a machine-gun, several signallers, two company runners and two Battalion runners. Each of the companies worked independently. 'B' and 'D' Companies were to hold the first trench. 'A' Company arrived in position well up to time and by 3.40 a.m. the whole Battalion was in position. Ernest established contact with 'B', 'C' and 'D' Companies, who were also in position. He then sent off runners to Battalion head-quarters with his report of the safe arrival of the different Companies in their respective positions. He passed word along for 'A' Company officers and N.C.O.s to attend for consultation and a final study of the maps. 'A' Company now had to lie in its trench for two hours before kick-off at Zero hour, 5.30 a.m.

By this point the original planning for the functions of the different companies had been thoroughly revised, and the rôle of 'A' Company redesignated. The front that the Battalion had to cover was so great that instead of 'A' Company remaining in reserve, each Company was now given a portion of front to itself: 'B' Company to the left, 'A' Company in the centre, 'C' Company to the right and 'D' to the extreme right. Each Company was responsible for one hundred yards of front, each man being eight yards from his neighbour on either side and the first and second waves starting at the same time from the first and second trenches. The men of the first wave and the men of the second wave were each made up in units consisting of four bombers or hand grenadiers, one N.C.O., four rifle grenadiers and about thirty-six infantry depending on the strength of the company, with a commissioned officer in the centre, then the four rifle grenadiers, the one non-commissioned officer and the four bombers. There was a machine-gun in the centre of 'A' Company operated by Sergeant Dow under the instructions of an officer.

Five minutes before Zero hour (5.25 a.m.) Ernest passed the word that bayonets were to be fixed and that the Battalion was to be ready for the signal for stepping off; the signal he told them was 'mine to be exploded on our right'.

Sir Philip Gibbs in his Dispatch of April 9th described the situation:

Today at dawn our armies began a battle which, if Fate has any kindness for the world, may be the beginning of the last great battles of the war. Our troops attacked on a wide front, including the Vimy Ridge – that grim hill which dominates the plain of Douai and the coalfields of Lens – and the German positions around Arras. In spite of bad fortune in the weather at the beginning of the day, so bad that there was no visibility for the airmen, and our men had to struggle forward in a heavy rain-storm, the first attacks have been successful, and the enemy has lost much ground, falling back in retreat to strong rear-guard lines where he is now fighting desperately.

The line of our attack covers a front of some twelve miles southwards from Givenchy-en-Gohelle, and is a sledge-hammer blow threatening to break the northern end of the

Hindenburg line, already menaced round St Quentin. As soon as the enemy was forced to retreat from that country east of Bapaume and Péronne, in order to escape a decisive blow on that line, he hurried up divisions and guns northwards to counter our attack there, while he prepared a new line of defence known as the Wotan line, as the southern part of the Hindenburg line, which joins it, is known as the Siegfried position, after two great heroes of old German mythology. He hoped to escape there before our new attack was ready, but we have been too quick for him, and his own plans were frustrated. So today began another titanic conflict which the world will hold its breath to watch, because of all that hangs upon it.

I have seen the fury of this beginning, and all the sky on fire with it, the most tragic and frightful sight that men have ever seen, with an infernal splendour beyond words to tell. The bombardment which went before the infantry assault lasted for several days, and reached a great height yesterday, when, coming from the south, I saw it for the first time. I went up in darkness long before light broke today to watch the opening of the battle. It was very cold, with a sharp wind blowing from the south-east and rain-squalls. The roads were quiet until I drew near to Arras, and then onwards there was the traffic of marching men going up to the fighting-lines, and of their transport columns, and of many ambulances. In darkness there were hundreds of little red lights, the glow of cigarette ends.

I went to a place a little outside Arras on the west side. It was not quite dark, because there was a kind of suffused light from the hidden moon, so that I could see the black mass of the cathedral city, the storm-centre of this battle, and away behind me to the left the tall, broken towers of Mont-St-Eloi, white and ghostly looking, across to the Vimy Ridge. The bombardment was now in full blast. It was a beautiful and devilish thing, and the beauty of it, and not the evil of it, put a spell upon one's senses. All our batteries, too many to count, were firing, and thousands of gun-flashes were winking and blinking from the hollows and hiding-places, and all their shells were rushing through the sky as though flocks of great birds were in flight, and all were bursting over German positions, with long flames, which rent the darkness and waved sword-blades of quivering light along the ridges. The earth opened, and pools of red fire gushed out. Star-shells burst magnificently, pouring down golden rain. Mines exploded east and west of Arras, and in a wide sweep from Vimy Ridge to Blangy southwards, and voluminous clouds, all bright with a glory of infernal fire, rolled up to the sky. The wind blew strongly across, beating back the noise of guns, but the air was filled with the deep roar and the slamming knocks of single heavies and the drum-fire of field-guns.

The first attack was at 5.30. Officers were looking at their wrist watches, as on a day in July last year. The earth lightened. In rank grass, looking white and old, scrubs of barbed wire were black on it. A few minutes before 5.30 the guns almost ceased to fire, so that there was a strange solemn hush. We waited, and pulses beat faster than second-hands. 'They're away,' said a voice by my side. The bombardment broke out again with new and enormous effects of fire and sound. The enemy was shelling Arras heavily, and black shrapnel and high explosives came over from his lines. But our gun-fire was twenty times as great. Around the whole sweep of his lines green lights rose. They were signals of distress, and his men were calling for help. It was dawn now, but clouded and storm-swept. A few airmen came out with the wind tearing at their wings, but they could see nothing in the mist and driven rain.

Fifteen minutes afterwards, groups of men came back. They were British wounded and German prisoners. They were met on the roadside by medical officers, who patched them up there and then before they were taken to the field-hospitals in ambulances. From these men, hit by shrapnel and machine-gun bullets, I heard the first news of progress. They were bloody and exhausted, but claimed success.

Ernest's soldier-servant was Private Black. He had joined the army in May 1916 and after two months' training in Dunfermline and three months in Nigg went to France on 29 December 1916. He was appointed as Ernest's servant on 30 March 1917, very shortly before the offensive began. He was to give a graphic account of the action:

> Over we go at 5.30 a.m., Captain Reid in advance. The noise was indescribable, the barrage fairly going; hell let loose, men falling over barbed wire in shell holes, wounded and killed. What an awful sight! Still on we go. Fifteen yards to our right Lieutenant Cuthbert is down wounded and dies from the effects within 25 yards of our own trench. Mr Reid still leads the way, encouraging the boys to advance and holding in check rash members of our company from going too far as they were in danger from our own barrage.

The creeping barrage (devised by Field Marshal Lord Alanbrooke, as he was later to be, Chief of the Imperial General Staff for most of the Second World War and, to my mind, a strategist who has not received quite his due for his part in shaping the plans which won that war) was a feature of trench warfare from at least 1916: but it was used as a critical tactical element for the first time at Arras. It consisted of a moving pattern of bombardment behind which the infantry advanced. In theory it should have worked well, but there were serious practical difficulties. It had attractions that seemed self-evident, and was still being used in the Second World War; but in conjunction with slow-moving infantry units it slowed down advances that were already slow and imposed inflexibility on tactics that already lacked fluidity. Nivelle was to set great store by it a week later at the Battle of the

Aisne, but it failed him there as it failed others on other occasions. There was no direct communication between the artillery pieces in the rear and the advancing infantry, so there was a risk either that the barrage would move ahead so fast that it provided no real protection to the troops as they advanced, or that it would move too slowly and that they would be killed by friendly fire. In the absence of radio communications between the artillery and advanced observers, as would be used in the Second World War, the only solution was to regulate the pace of advance by meticulous timekeeping: the infantry was expected to advance at a rate of fifty yards a minute. A barrage was targeted on a particular trench line and was then 'lifted' at the moment when it was thought the troops would have reached that target. If they had fallen behind, it would be lifted too soon, so that the advancing troops were faced by fire from re-occupied and freshly defended trenches. The requirement to move at a predetermined rate in this way was dangerously rigid. No account could be taken of problems that the infantry met as they moved ahead; conversely, they could not take advantage of success to push forward faster than they had planned.

The Company moved forward steadily at a walking pace. There were shell bursts quite close from a German barrage which began just one minute after the attack was launched, from which Ernest received a small piece of shrapnel in the upper right thigh, near the top of his leg. The wound was not deep and about the size, as Private Black described it, of a sixpence or a shilling (about the size of a five or ten pence piece). At about the same time Private Black himself received a scratch on the back of his leg below the knee. Neither of the wounds appeared to be serious at this stage. Private Black bound up Ernest's wound with a field dressing and they continued.

The Company had now reached one of a number of railway lines that crossed the very level ground of the plain at this stage. Private Black's platoon was in the centre of the advance and Ernest along with the platoon walked along the railway towards the Black Line. The rest of 'A' Company was extended on either flank. The position was obviously a very exposed one and Ernest had much work to do in keeping each flank in as straight a line as possible.

Eventually at about 5.45 a.m. the enemy front trenches and the Black Line were reached. So far there had been few casualties, not more than fifty-nine in all, mostly caused by the German barrage which had injured Ernest and Private Black and which resulted in fifty-four casualties amongst the other ranks, one officer killed and four wounded, among them, as Private Black described, Ernest's friend, D. W. H. Cuthbert (who died of his wounds later that day).

An hour and twenty-five minutes were spent at the Black Line, when consolidation was at once begun and preparations were made to continue the attack. The precision of the timing is interesting and was of course dictated by the need to co-ordinate movements with the barrage and also with the plans for the movement of successive bodies of troops. Ernest was busy rushing around giving orders to 'A' Company officers and men to dig themselves in on Fred's Wood, the part of the first objective which they were to secure. Then he was back at the German dug-outs where the moppers-up had turned out prisoners. He gave orders that the prisoners were not to be killed, but sent back to the British lines. Then he was off locating snipers, getting machine-guns in position and sending back runners to Battalion Headquarters to report that the first object had been gained.

This must have been about the last opportunity that Ernest had to study the ground ahead of him and he may have had the glimpse of Monchy which Sergeant Whiteman of the 10th Royal Fusiliers was to get in the afternoon of the same day from a position near the Brown Line; the memory was to stay with him:

Two miles off, over the undulating grassy country and beyond the Brown Line, could be seen a village crowning the summit of a circular hill, with its red roofed cottages peeping out from amongst the green foliage of trees – altogether a very picturesque view. The village was Monchy, our objective. There is something fascinating about the first sight – from a distance at least – of a position one has to capture; it makes one conjecture as to the future, if it does nothing else.

At this stage Ernest said to Private Black that it appeared that they were now in the first wave and not the second, as he could not see the leader of the first wave and his platoon. It turned out later that this had been the position from the start: the leader of the first wave later reported that his men had been in position one hundred yards to the rear of Ernest and his men. The ground had been cut up with crater holes; the men had to find a way round as best they could. They got mixed up and those who faced most obstacles found their way to the rear.

Ernest was very energetic, dashing all over the place and sorting out problems. Private Black said later that his leg must have been sore, as the bandage was always slipping down and having to be hitched up, but when he offered to retie it Ernest told him that it was all right.

Orders were sent back to Lieutenant Callan, the leader of what had been the first wave, that when it was time to move off he was to join Ernest's men, as the first wave had been sadly thinned.

At five minutes to Zero hour the men fastened spades and shovels on their backs for use at the next objective and were told to load their rifles. At Zero hour, 7.10 a.m., the advance began again behind a creeping barrage. The objective now was the Blue Line, the rising ground known as 'Observation Ridge'. The advance was more difficult now. There were more dug-outs containing German troops to be bombed, and stiff resistance was met. Ernest and 'A' Company came across German soldiers whom they attempted to detain or send back and who, in accordance with his orders, were not killed. Ernest rallied his men: he called to them to come on and he walked ahead to encourage them.

The Battalion's objective on the Blue Line was known as 'Railway Triangle'. The whole area to this side of the suburbs of

Arras was, as it still is, a maze of railway lines and embankments, used partly by passenger trains and partly by industrial freight. The Triangle represented a cutting in the middle of three inter-secting railway lines. The lines were elevated on embankments, and a frontal attack on the Triangle could not fail to be dangerous. Apart from the problems presented by the topography, between the Triangle and Monchy lay Feuchy Chapel, which the *Official History* describes as 'a veritable fortress'. The ground today has changed little since 1917, and the vulnerability of Railway Triangle, which the Battalion had to take, and in which the time–table required it to stay for some time, is easily understood. As 'A' Company approached the Triangle, the advance became slower and slower. Ernest and Private Black were always in advance. Ernest sent Black off to carry messages, and detailed him to carry out various other orders. Eventually the Battalion was held up along a line running north and south through the centre of the Railway Triangle. There were German dug-outs on the inner sides of two of the railway lines, and from the embankments machine-gun and rifle fire enfiladed the ground over which the 44th Brigade had to advance. Snipers were active and the Battalion was a sitting target as long as it was stuck in the middle of the Triangle.

At about 10 a.m. Private Black looked round to find Ernest sitting on a stone or something of the sort, holding his thumbs one on each side of his right thigh about four or five inches below the earlier wound. A bullet had gone in on the right side, cut through the artery and come out on the left. Blood was flowing profusely from the two ends of the wound.

Lieutenant Callan was now part of the first wave with Ernest, and he and others wanted to move him back to a dug-out or shelter. Private Black stoutly resisted any movement until the wound was bound up. He saw that if Ernest were moved before something was done about the wound he would almost certainly bleed to death. Ernest agreed to let Private Black bind up his wound. Black told him to lie back just where he was, although the ground was in a frightful state as a result of the rain that had been falling throughout the advance. With some help from Lieutenant Callan, Black got Ernest's wounds bound up and then he and some of the men carried him back a short distance to what shelter from enfilading fire the old German trenches could afford. There was now an opportunity to attend to the wounds properly without the danger incidental to remaining in open ground, but they could find no R.A.M.C. men. Fortunately, Private Black had received first-aid lessons before he joined up and he tied a cloth above the artery, inserted a shilling in the cloth and twisted it as an improvised tourniquet. The bleeding was arrested entirely although by this time Ernest had lost a large amount of blood.

By the time Ernest was hit, he had advanced three-quarters of a mile from the front line. The journey, which had taken four and a half hours and was to cost him his life, was shorter than Tom's daily stroll to his office.

In the meantime many other men, and particularly officers, were hit by the fire to which they had been so exposed. As well as Ernest, another five officers were hit, including Lieutenant Callan. A bullet hit him on the shoulder as he was turning and ploughed a fairly deep wound in both shoulders although missing his spine, because of the angle of his turn. The Battalion was pinned down in the Triangle for three hours. Artillery support was called up, and eventually, with the assistance of a tank and the support battalion, 7th Camerons, the Triangle was secured at 12.30, and the advance moved to the Blue Line, where it consolidated without attracting enemy fire. At 2.20 p.m. 46th Brigade went through the Line and a few hours later the 9th Battalion was relieved by 7th Camerons and went back to Reserve. Brown Line was captured by 5.30 p.m.

The Regimental history says that, 'The operation had been entirely successful and had been accomplished without undue loss'. The Battalion had captured over 200 prisoners, four machine-guns, one trench mortar and some mining instruments. It is not clear whether the Battalion ever did reach its final objective, the Brown Line, and it appears from its History that it did not, and that 46th Brigade may have done so. In any event the overall objective, the capture of Monchy-le-Preux by 37th Division, was not achieved. The 9th Battalion itself was ordered forward to Feuchy, where it remained all day in reserve for the attack on Monchy, but it returned that night to Arras to be billeted in cellars in the Grande Place. From there it moved to Schram Barracks, where it received the congratulations of the Commander-in-Chief, and the Army, Corps and Divisional Commanders. Before it left Arras the Battalion was to fight on many occasions with conspicuous gallantry.

In the course of its time at Arras, the Battalion lost 495 officers and men, killed, missing or wounded. The Battalion historian seems almost embarrassed by what were low rates of casualty at Arras and on the Somme (488) compared to the losses at Loos in 1915, when the figure was over 600. He asks himself why this is so. 'The spirit and fighting will of the Battalion was unquestionably the same on all three occasions.' The reason was partly that there had been no creeping barrage at Loos: he reckoned that its use at Arras had limited losses. But the principal explanation was that at Loos there had been no limit on objectives. Indeed the order to the Division was to 'push on to the full extent of its power'. On the Somme and subsequently, one battalion was given a specific task, and when that was accomplished another went through to the next objective. This was the doctrine of 'bite and hold'. The lesson of Loos had been that 'however gallant the company officers and other ranks, they could not be expected to achieve the impossible'.

There was indeed a difficult balance to achieve, which was never attained in the Great War. Experience showed that no unit could sustain an infantry advance for more than a very limited distance in the conditions of the Western Front. On the other hand, a strictly defined objective made it impossible to exploit success. The dilemma was rooted in the fact that while technical advances in warfare had rendered cavalry obsolete, mechanised vehicles and radio communications had not yet come of age.

It is worth mentioning one of the officers who was killed in the course of the Easter Monday advance. Captain H. J. Collins was the Roman Catholic Chaplain to the Brigade and was attached to the Black Watch. Some of the chaplains in the Great War were towering figures who inspired immense affection amongst the men. Many of them, too, were affected by the experience in a way that was to remain with them for the rest of their lives. Those who commanded most respect were frequently the Roman Catholic chaplains, who seem to have shared the risks of their men to an enormous degree. The loss of Captain Collins was felt by the whole Battalion. He had joined it before it left Britain and he was vastly proud of his attachment. In every tour in the trenches he was with the Battalion and his position was always in the Front Line, with a haversack full of cigarettes which were his personal gift to the men. He carried out impromptu funeral services for those killed, even in the Front Line, sometimes under rifle and machine-gun fire. He was a cheery man who heartened all ranks by his presence – particularly when conditions were bad. He had been recommended for the Military Cross some months before he died and two months after his death he was mentioned in Dispatches.

Two of the First World War poets were present at Arras. Edward Thomas, a Second Lieutenant in the Artists' Rifles, was killed in action on 9 April. Siegfried Sassoon was there too. He had been moving towards the Front since leaving Rouen on 11 March. He was to have his 'breakdown' and make his public protest against the war in early July, but already he was under stress. He had lost his belief in the war. He wrote of himself in the third person: 'He doesn't know for what he is making the sacrifice; he has no passion for England, except as a place of pleasant land-scapes and comfortable towns. He despises the English point of view and British complacency. Some day he will be able to explain this feeling of unreasonable acquiescence'. As he approached the Front, the acquiescence seemed to prevail over the resentment. He reached Basseux, seven miles from Arras, on Easter Sunday, but he was not in the first wave, and when the battle began the following day he was safe in a dug-out, reading *Far from the Madding Crowd*. In the second phase of the attack, on 14 April, he was on the Hindenburg Line, writing in his diary: 'At 9.30, sitting in the Hindenburg underground tunnel on Sunday night, fully expecting to get killed on Monday morning'. He was not killed, but was hit on his right shoulder, an injury which was to take him back to England, to his protest, and then on to Scotland and Craiglockhart War Hospital, and Dr W. H. R. Rivers, and a meeting with the patient in an adjoining room:

> There was a gentle knock on the door of my room and a young officer entered. Short, dark-haired, shyly hesitant, he stood for a moment before coming across to the window, where I was sitting on my bed cleaning my golf clubs. A favourable first impression was made by the fact that he had under his arm several copies of The Old Huntsman. He had come, he said, hoping that I would be so gracious as to inscribe them for himself and some of his friends.
>
> He spoke with a slight stammer, which was no unusual thing in that neurosis-pervaded hospital. My leisurely, commentative method of inscribing the books enabled him to feel more at home with me. He had a charming honest smile, and his manners – he stood at my elbow rather as though conferring with a superior officer – were modest and ingratiating. He gave me the names of his friends first. When it came to his own I found myself writing one that has since gained a notable place in the roll of English poets – Wilfred Owen.

Arras is not the most remembered of First World War battles, but Sassoon ensured its commemoration by a poem he wrote before the battle, entitled *The General*: its rhyme and metre are impeccable, but the sentiments are a little facile (and indeed it is said that the inspiration for the verse lay in a sighting of Sir Ivor Maxse, one of the 'better' First War generals):

> 'Good morning, Good morning!' the General said
> When we met him last week on our way to the line.

Now the soldiers he smiled at are most of 'em dead,
And we're cursing his staff for incompetent swine.
'He's a cheery old card,' grunted Harry to Jack
As they slogged up to Arras with rifle and pack.
But he did for them both by his plan of attack.

We left Ernest in relative shelter from enemy fire in a German trench, with his leg in a tourniquet, suffering from the shock and pain of two wounds and having lost a considerable amount of blood. Here there was a wait for over two-and-a-half hours before a start could be made for the third objective. 'A' Company found that its right and left flanks had been held up 100 yards in their rear. This left them in an even more exposed position than the configuration of the ground had caused. They could not move until the two wings had joined up with them and in the meantime their flanks were exposed to the enemy.

Astonishingly, in these circumstances, the resourceful Private Black now proceeded to make beef tea in his can over a candle. Such devotion to duty and kindness to Ernest can hardly be comprehended: even to think of preparing a hot drink while the Battalion was pinned down with little or no cover, exposed to sniper and shell fire and shrapnel bursts that continued to wound and kill men all around him, beggars belief. But the beef tea was an ideal antidote to shock and the effects of loss of blood. It warmed them both up and Ernest was in good spirits, taking a keen interest in the position of the Company.

At last, to their relief, the barrage started again and the attack began on the third position. At this stage the Commanding Officer, Colonel Innes, came up and reviewed the position. He was to report that when he saw Ernest at this stage 'he was very weak from loss of blood but his spirits were excellent and he knew he had done well and that his Company had taken many prisoners'.

Colonel Innes got hold of a medical officer and a stretcher. Black used four German prisoners as stretcher bearers and they made their way back over the pitted and rutted ground, through a mosaic of shell holes to the outskirts of Arras and the first-aid post of 15th Division, two miles back from where he had been wounded: the two miles must have taken a long time and this in the freezing rain, sleet and snow.

Ernest's leg was examined to see if any blood was oozing from the wound, but Private Black's peacetime first-aid lessons had been learned well, and as the bleeding had been stopped the dressing was not touched. After a fairly short wait Ernest was taken by two further German prisoners to a Casualty Clearing Station in an old factory in the centre of Arras, where he arrived at 2 p.m. Private Black, whose loyalty to Ernest, to whom he had only been appointed as batman ten days earlier, was outstanding, was still with him. At the Casualty Clearing Station they were inclined not to do anything to Ernest's wound, but he, no doubt knowing how dirty the conditions had been, asked them to take off the bandage and put on a fresh dressing. This was done and he then fell asleep and lay there till about 6 p.m., when with three other stretcher cases he was taken in a motor ambulance, with Private Black on the outside, to Duisans and 41st Casualty Clearing Station. Ernest's dressings were again replaced and here he remained until Thursday 13 April. The hospital consisted of a canvas marquee with wooden huts as wards. What the conditions were like, one can only imagine, but Private Black recorded that the weather outside was bitterly cold and snowy. At about 2 a.m. on Wednesday 12 April an operation was carried out 'under chloroform' and some 'bad flesh' (gangrene) was removed. Black saw him later that morning between 7 a.m. and 8 a.m. and Ernest was in good spirits. He was confident that he was going to live, although he appreciated that he might lose his leg. On Thursday 13 April he was sent off from Duisans by train. Private Black was told that he was going to Boulogne and from there would be taken to England. The matron of the Clearing Station confirmed Ernest's views and told Private Black that his life would be spared but that his leg might be lost.

Private Black never saw Ernest again. Black was very properly awarded the Distinguished Conduct Medal for the bravery that he had displayed in carrying Ernest to shelter in most dangerous circumstances and dressing his wounds. Colonel Innes also commended Black's gallantry in a letter to Tom eleven days after the battle.

Black is another of the unnoticed heroes of the Great War, and it would be good to know more of this man who did so much for Ernest. The answer to the most important question is affirmative: he will make one further appearance in this story, and we know that happily he *did* survive the war. Beyond that I discovered little. His War Office army service record was not preserved.

The Regimental records give some slight biographical details, and a Christian name: Alexander. Alexander Black was a volunteer, like Ernest, enlisting at Forfar on 9 May 1916. The Battalion's War Diary tells us that his D. C. M. was awarded as early as 10 May 1917 as an 'Immediate Reward' for his conduct on 9 April. The citation, which was gazetted on 18 June, reads: 'For conspicuous gallantry and devotion to duty. He went to the assistance of a wounded officer and in spite of the most intense hostile fire succeeded in carrying him to a place of safety'.

What surprised me was his age. He was 36 when he enlisted, almost old enough at Arras to be Ernest's father, and could not have done more if Ernest *had* been his son. Alexander Black was a brave and a good man.

11

The Darkness of the Grave

Ernest's journey on the hospital train must have been the stuff of nightmare. The train, blacked out to avoid attracting enemy fire, was full of seriously injured men. Ernest, weak from all he had undergone and with the pain of his two wounds exacerbated by surgery, was almost certainly feverish. Modern painkillers were not available. The distance the train had to travel was only some 45 miles, but in wartime conditions, without lights, and on lines that had to be improvised to replace those that had been cut by artillery shells, the journey took many hours. Outside, the sky was full of sleet and snow, but it was lit up from time to time by the flashes of guns and rifles, Verey lights and star-shells. All the time there was the crash of heavy artillery, the crackling of rifle fire and the hammer of machine-guns. The initial part of the journey was never far from the Front Line.

He did not arrive at his destination until Friday morning. Private Black had been misinformed: that destination was not Boulogne, but No. 1 Red Cross Hospital (Duchess of Westminster's) at Le Touquet, close to Paris-Plage.

Le Touquet, its accessibility to Paris recognised by the name given to its beach, was a very exclusive resort from the end of the nineteenth century until at least the Second World War, but particularly so in the early years of the twentieth century, before the south of France became a fashionable alternative. The landscape surrounding the town is distinctive, with extensive pine forests and gentle hills, and was well adapted to the aristocratic pursuit, as it then was, of golf. The beach is of high-quality sand stretching for miles beside the Opal Coast, but there was no need for the rich and famous to get sand in their shoes: elevated wooden walkways between the sand and the town allowed them to take their exercise and to see and be seen. Boudin's painting of *L'Empresse Eugénie à Trouville* gives some idea of the elegance of a similar resort, although painted before the end of the Second Empire. Even today Le Touquet has an air of distinction that marks it out from the other watering places along the coast. The architecture of the town, as would be expected, is noteworthy, and a number of celebrated architects have contributed to its diversity.

From the first, there was a strong British presence and Constance, the Duchess of Westminster, had a beautiful house, a bell-gabled villa in extensive gardens, in the town. Constance was the wife of 'Bendor', Duke of Westminster. They were amongst the leaders of European society, and the Duke, who was a close friend of Churchill, was reputed to be the richest man in Europe. Constance was the second Duke's first wife, but not his last duchess. He had no fewer than four, and his third, Loelia, is still remembered for saying, 'Anyone seen in a bus over the age of 30 cannot be counted a success in life'.

Several aristocratic ladies founded hospitals in France for the wounded of the First World War and Constance's, at Le Touquet, was one of the most famous. There the first case of shellshock was to be reported.

Either on his arrival at Le Touquet or, more probably, at the field hospital in Arras, it had been found that the bullet that had severed the artery in Ernest's leg had also smashed the bone. He now underwent a further operation on the evening of Friday 13 April to retie the artery. Again, it was thought to be worth recording that the operation was performed under chloroform. The availability of chloroform and the awareness of the need to maintain aseptic conditions were the only significant features that distinguished military medicine in 1917 from what was practised at Waterloo.

By this stage, Ernest's condition was poor and he was not expected to survive. On 13 April (the day that Ernest arrived at Le Touquet) Tom and Annie received a telegram:

REGRET TO INFORM YOU 2 LT TE REID BLACK WATCH WAS
WOUNDED APRIL NINTH. DETAILS WIRED WHEN RECEIVED.

This would be one of the two telegrams that everyone at home dreaded. One can imagine the icy grasp at their hearts when Tom and Annie saw the telegram boy at the doorstep.

An even more ominous telegram arrived in Paisley at 7.10 p.m. on the same evening:

YOU ARE PERMITTED TO VISIT 2ND LT TE REID BLACK WATCH DANGEROUSLY ILL GUNSHOT WOUNDS RIGHT THIGH AT 1 RED CROSS HOSPITAL LETOUQUET [sic] YOU MUST PRODUCE THIS TELEGRAM AT WAR OFFICE OFFICERS CASUALTY DEPT FOR EXCHANGE FOR PERMIT. IT YOU WISH TO SUBSTITUTE ANOTHER NAME FOR VISIT YOUR WRITTEN AUTHORITY SANCTIONING SUBSTITUTE MUST BE ATTACHED TO TELEGRAM. IF YOU ARE UNABLE TO BEAR EXPENSE TO LONDON TAKE THIS TELEGRAM TO NEAREST POLICE STATION.

There now took place what I have always regarded as perhaps the most poignant episode in the whole of this sad story. Tom and Annie went from Paisley to Ernest's bedside in Le Touquet. That is not surprising. What is surprising is that they travelled by air. They may have been modern-minded enough to have a washing machine and an electric potato peeler at home in Hazelwood, but there is something almost surreal in a journey across the Channel in a heavier-than-air flying machine by this provincial couple. It is worth reflecting on how alien they must have found the whole episode. They were not untravelled: their honeymoon backpacking had been followed by other foreign holidays; but these holidays were taken essentially in the way that people had taken holidays for a hundred years. Annie and Tom would have seen motor cars and may well have travelled in one, but they would not, I think, have one of their own, and indeed I suspect that they never did. They would have read of aeroplanes, but it must be questionable whether they had ever seen one and I do not suppose that they knew anyone who had flown in one.

In 1917 Tom was aged 58 and Annie 54, but in those years, in dress and demeanour and in attitudes of mind, it was required by decorum and convention that people looked, as indeed in their views and outlook they were, much older than their ages would suggest today. However, this staid and sober couple, he I imagine dressed in a morning suit and she in discreetly dark clothes, perhaps with a veil, took to the air to be with their son. They had not reported to the nearest police station to obtain a travel warrant to London, but when they reached the War Office, Tom signed a declaration prepared for him on War Office paper to the effect that he was not in a position to pay for fares for the flight to Le Touquet. That declaration would be accurate enough to allow Tom to sign it with a clear conscience; he could not have envisaged when he left Paisley by train that his journey was to be completed by air.

He and Annie received permits and travelling warrants and reached No. 1 Red Cross Hospital at Le Touquet on Saturday 14 April, just a day after Ernest had himself arrived.

In the early hours of Monday morning of that same week, Ernest had been a fit young 20-year-old, full of vitality and rising to the challenge of the responsibilities that had been so early thrust on him. The whole potential that lay in his ability and his vitality was cancelled in an instant when a German bullet hit his leg. He had endured the pain and makeshift facilities of the dressing station and the field hospital and now he was in a hospital bed, with his parents incongruously beside him. It is hard to imagine the meeting without emotion.

Even before he had been moved to Le Touquet, Ernest had managed to write to his parents. Characteristically, he minimised the gravity of his wounds, and his letters were full of hope. Equally, when his parents arrived, only a few hours after they had been summoned, he made light of his condition. Indeed he was a little better, and he told Tom and Annie that he felt a fraud and that they had been brought there under false pretences.

Family tradition as it had been passed to Elsie had Tom and Annie arriving in the morning, finding Ernest better than they had expected, going for lunch with the Matron and returning from lunch to find him dead. Events were not quite so cruel. They were with him for five days. Their presence must have been enormously welcome to Ernest and it must have been a solace afterwards to Tom and Annie that they had been able to be with him, share his last few days and make his end less solitary than that of many other wounded men.

They brought him news of home. They told him that Jimmy Thomson, the family friend who described Tom to me eighty years later, was coming out soon. (By this stage of the war the shortage of manpower was such that although he was not allowed to fight before his eighteenth birthday, Jimmy was called up and trained before that date. He came down the gangway on to French soil on his birthday.) Ernest's reaction was interesting. He told them this was good; more good men were needed in France. I find it instructive that in the circumstances in which he found himself he could look beyond his own predicament to speak in such terms; and that his attitude to the war had changed so little from the spirit in which he had volunteered. The war was still a clear-cut conflict between good and bad: more good men were needed to fight it.

Chloroform and antiseptics were important, but the third element that was to transform what was essentially nursing into twentieth-century medicine had not yet arrived: modern drugs, and in particular antibiotics. Despite all that antiseptic conditions could do, and despite the fact that with anaesthesia surgeons had time to perform intricate operations without causing suffering to their patients, the efforts of military doctors were again and again frustrated by the fact that wounds had been infected before casualties reached the Clearing Stations. Sir Alexander Fleming's claim to be the first pioneer in this field is disputed, but he was certainly up in front, and during the Great War he served in a military hospital in France and saw how little doctors could do against an infected wound. He had already worked in the bacteriology laboratory at St Mary's, London and he returned there after the war, determined to find a solution to the tragic problem he had encountered in France. The story is well known of his chance discovery, in 1928, of something growing on a glass plate that had been left unwashed in his laboratory sink and of the airborne spore that had landed on it and colonised, and cleared a mould. For various reasons Fleming lost confidence in his discovery and it was Florey and Chain who developed it. The first patient to be treated with penicillin was a policeman in Oxford in 1941. Although he has a place in medical history because his condition improved immediately he was given the drug, the outcome was less than satisfactory from his point of view: the supply ran out and he relapsed and died. But the effectiveness of the drug had been established. At first it was reserved exclusively for the armed forces and it saved tens, perhaps hundreds, of thousands of lives in the Second World War.

Annie lived through that War, and she must have needed all her charity not to resent the fact that the new wonder drugs, the sulphonamides (which are bacteriostatic, merely preventing the multiplication of certain bacteria, and are prone to resistance, as well as provoking toxic reactions) and penicillin (which is a more effective, bacteriocidal agent), had not been available a generation earlier.

Ironically the bacterial culture which was killed entirely by chance on the unwashed glass plate in 1928 was a culture of septicaemia, precisely the organism which was attacking Ernest. Private Black knew all about blood poisoning, not only from his civilian first-aid training but because he too unfortunately suffered blood poisoning in the leg which was hit at the same time as Ernest received his first wound. Black's leg swelled from the knee up to double its usual size and he had to go to one hospital after another. Fortunately he recovered, but he was lucky to do so, as his septicaemia must have been close to spreading through his whole system. In his opinion it was likely that it was Ernest's first wound that was poisoned, as he recalled that Ernest's hands and his own were very muddy when the wound had been dressed. They obviously had no means of washing their hands, which were in contact with Ernest's leg; and he thought it probable that they conveyed germs into the wound. From the fact that he volunteered this information and suggestion I tend to think that he must have known that the wound was very dirty indeed. Ernest's kilt was not muddy at the time and only became so when he lay down to get his second wound dressed.

Initially the doctors had been minded to amputate the leg. Only with hindsight can this be seen to be the procedure which should have been followed. There was at first some improvement in Ernest's condition and by the time he was seriously ill the septicae-mia would have invaded his whole system; finally he was probably suffering from what would now be called multi-organ failure.

On the morning of Wednesday 18 April, four days after his parents arrived, Ernest may indeed have been feeling a little better. Although the family tradition of the arrival of Tom and Annie, Ernest's relapse and death within a single day is wrong in its compression, I see no reason to reject it in its entirety. They may well have had lunch with the matron on that Wednesday. The accounts do not say whether they were beside him when he died, but die he did, peacefully, at four that afternoon. Tom and Annie were comforted by the Duchess of Westminster. She said an interesting thing to Annie: 'Go and buy a hat, my dear'. Was she being appallingly insensitive? Not at all, and Tom and Annie knew that. She was giving the best sort of advice she could in such circumstances. People who have just been bereaved find it difficult to cope with sympathy and the best thing that can happen to them is to have to immerse themselves in mundane, necessary tasks. Annie was going to have to attend a funeral, and the conventions of those days required that she wear a suitable hat on such an occasion, certainly with a heavy veil. If she had to go into town, find a hat, talk to shopkeepers and keep up a brave front, that would carry her through a few hours at least, and for that reason the Duchess's words were always remembered with gratitude.

Fortunately Tom and Annie did not have the strain of a long wait in the alien surroundings of Le Touquet before the funeral took place. It was held just 48 hours after Ernest had died.

What was described as a touching service took place in a little wooden chapel at Étaples, conducted by the Rev. Mr W. Phin Gillieson, of Ayr, and the Rev. Mr Jolland of Northumberland, CF. It was good that a Scottish minister was there.

Ernest was buried in Grave A 192 in the Military Cemetery at Étaples at 11 a.m. in the presence of Annie and Tom, some friends he had made in the hospital, and a military party.

The earliest photograph (Fig. 13) of the grave which I have was, I suspect, taken at that time, perhaps for Tom and Annie. The British government had made the decision that those who died in France should be buried there and remain there, and the photograph would be dear to them. It shows a narrow grave, defined and elevated by four concrete sides, which retain unplanted and recently raked soil. At the top is a stout but simple wooden cross on which punched metal tapes have been tacked, presumably with Ernest's name, regiment and service number embossed. A later photograph shows the cemetery in more or less its present form. Contemporary eyewitnesses found the original cemetery, in all it simplicity, even more moving than its grander successor. I do not know whether Ernest's body was moved from the primitive grave shown in the first photograph. There is now no longer an elevated grave or a concrete surround. The graves are level with the grass that runs between them and they are marked by the plain but beautiful headstones which are familiar from all the Commonwealth War Graves. The words on the headstone read:

CAPTAIN
THOMAS ERNEST REID
THE BLACK WATCH
18th April 1917

Below that is carved a cross and below are the further words:

AGED 20
HE FOUGHT A GOOD FIGHT

When another photograph was taken the cemetery was still in the course of construction. The flowers and grass look a little unkempt and scaffolding is erected round the two cenotaphs of stone. The photograph looks as if it was taken in the early 1920s. A single flower has been planted on Ernest's grave and a card is attached to it. I don't know who planted the flower or took the photograph. There is a beautiful oil painting in the Imperial War Museum of *The Cemetery, Étaples* painted by Sir John Lavery in 1919, which shows the burial ground at this stage in its evolution.

A further photograph is of a much more established grave. A beautiful rose is growing on the grave. Shrubs have been planted. The grass is well tended. This photograph was, I think, taken by Elsie's friend, Betty Murchie, in the 1930s when she was on holiday in France, and brought back by her for Ronald.

The final photograph I took myself in the 1990s, when I visited the cemetery with my family.

The Military Cemetery designed by Sir Edwin Lutyens is in the sand dunes near the railway, overlooking the site of 'the Bullring'. I had visited many of the First World War cemeteries which are, sadly, profusely scattered over this part of France, from relatively small ones to the huge Lutyens Memorial at Thiepval which inspired Charles Chilton, but I was surprised by the emotional reaction I experienced when I visited Étaples. Of course there was the personal element: here my own uncle was buried; this was as close as I would ever be to a physical encounter with the man of whose presence I had been aware for so long. But there was more to it than that. First, there is the size – it is the biggest Commonwealth War Graves Cemetery in France, and in it over 11,000 men are buried. The sheer number of headstones commemorating young men needlessly dead, some of them Germans as well as British, inspires awe. Then there is the configuration of the

Cemetery. Most of the war cemeteries, astonishingly, achieve a certain informality. There are some that have the feel of a garden at home. Roses grow round graves – thistles in some of the Scottish cemeteries – and although they are meticulously maintained, part of the skill has been to give at least the illusion of unplanned artistry. The result is to create some of the peace and reassurance of an English country churchyard. At Étaples, on the other hand, though the flowers, the grass, the shrubs are there, there is not the same informality. The graves are placed to face inwards in a hollow square. The two massive cenotaphs are bedecked with stone flags, and between them is a long stone daïs with the Stone of Remembrance at its mid-point. The Cross of Sacrifice, that beautiful emblem which dignifies all the cemeteries, is there but, despite that, the impression is of a regiment drawn up on parade before a saluting base. The military discipline which claimed these men's lives seems to hold them in its grasp even in death.

And again, on the two sides of the stone daïs, there is a book which shows where each man is buried. With that information a few words of biography appear. For Ernest these words are:

Captain Thomas Ernest Reid
'A' Coy. 3rd, Attd. 9th Bn, Black Watch (Royal Highlanders)
who died, Aged 20, on Wednesday 18 April, 1917.
Captain REID, Son of Thomas Fulton Reid (Solicitor),
and Mrs Annie A. Reid, of 'Hazelwood', Castlehead, Paisley.
Law Student at Glasgow University in civil life.

I was struck, first, by Ernest's age. Just over 20. He had done so much yet lived so little. What promise, what abilities lay unfulfilled. And I was struck too by the pathos in the reference to his other, civilian life and to his parents: to the whole other existence from which he had been torn to be left in this foreign soil, his life unlived, his potential unrealised. When I drove away from the cemetery I was close to tears.

On the morning of Thursday 19 April, the day between Ernest's death and the funeral, Tom had sent a telegram to their minister, the Rev. Mr R. E. Glendening, of Victoria Place Baptist Church. On Sunday 22 April, after preaching from Hebrews XI, 27: 'He endured as seeing Him who is invisible', Mr Glendening closed his address by telling the congregation of Ernest's death. He spoke of 'the stricken parents and brothers and friends – who form part of that great, growing company of bereaved in the land' and he spoke thus of Ernest and his death:

He fell in a noble cause. But the splendour of the sacrifice, while it helps us to bear the loss, does not change the sadness of the fact. We cannot but grieve that such a bright, beautiful, promising life – like so many others – had to be sacrificed through the unholy ambitions of a cruel militarism which today is deluging Europe with blood. Ernest Reid, as we best knew him, was an exceptionally fine lad in every sense, physically, mentally, and morally. As a law student at Glasgow University, his career was full of promise. There he joined the OTC, eventually receiving a commission, and finally joining the Army in France. Before going to France he resolved publicly to make his great confession of Christ, and it was my joy and privilege in June 1915, to baptise and receive him into the Church. As a soldier and a man he was esteemed both by his superiors and his men. He was not a warrior by instinct: but he heard the call of duty, and willingly offered himself in defence of home and native land. Great ideals moved him. And amid all the dangers and sufferings of this terrible war 'He endured as seeing Him who is invisible'. He found his courage and his comfort in God. That fact fills us with peace, today.

12

The Clouds that Gather
Round the Setting Sun

I do not remember if it was after Ernest's death or Tom's that Annie briefly turned to spiritualism, surprisingly for one of her background. It would not be strange if it was Ernest's loss that prompted such a reaction. Thousands of mothers tried to contact their dead sons in these years by this means. Robert Graves, in *Goodbye to All That,* described Siegfried Sassoon's mother doing just that, and although she was left in anonymity, Sassoon recognised the story. Always ready to take offence, he was infuriated by what he called the 'mental inflammation' aroused. He threatened legal action, and although Graves expressed surprise, the book was first published with blank spaces where the passage had been.

But even if there was no visitor from the Other Side, there were two unexpected callers at Hazelwood. The first was a young lady who introduced herself as someone who had been a close friend of Ernest (at university?) and with whom he might indeed have had an understanding. Annie was sceptical. Despite her air of innocence, I suspect she was a reasonably shrewd observer of the human race and, as her interest in the young ministers in Saltcoats showed, realistic about the interest of young people in the other sex. But children can be adept at concealing their emotional entanglements from their parents and Annie's maternal possessiveness may have inclined her to be doubtful. For Ernest's sake, if not for that of the girl, I like to think that she was his sweetheart and that in his all too short life his heart was touched by romance. It would be pleasing to think that in the cold, spiritual loneliness of the trenches his heart was warmed by the thoughts of a girl at home.

The other visitor was the indefatigable and loyal Private Black. He turned up and gave a long and very detailed account of Ernest's last days, which has formed a crucial part of this narrative. In these post-war days soldiers did appear, visiting the parents of deceased officers and giving accounts to their parents that owed more to the hope of reward than to accuracy. Tom and Annie were doubtful about the veracity of Private Black's statement. I recognise that Tom, an experienced lawyer, would have considerable ability in assessing the credibility of witnesses, but I am inclined to accept as accurate everything of moment that Black says. Where his descriptive language seems fulsome, I think that is due more to his background and reading matter than to a desire to gild the lily. If I were to be hyper-critical in relation to his first-aid activities, I could mention that a press report to which I refer below says that Sergeant Dow, whom Black does not mention in this connection, was one of those who rendered first aid and conveyed Ernest to a place of safety. I do not know, however, that Sergeant Dow's rôle was very important, as Colonel Innes's letter, written just eleven days after the battle, does not mention him. Colonel Innes does say that it was he, the Colonel, who 'got a medical officer to [Ernest] and had him carried down . . . [to] the field ambulance in safety'. Private Black assigned this critical rôle to himself plus his German prisoners. But these are not important matters, merely questions of detail or emphasis, and it is perfectly possible that Colonel Innes recalled the facts incorrectly or thought that it was appropriate that a Colonel should be making the arrangements rather than a soldier-servant.

There are in my view a number of cogent reasons for taking all that Private Black says at face value. First, his rôle in saving Ernest's life on the battlefield was recognised as a matter of record at a very early stage by other people, and was not cooked up by him later for the purpose of his visit to the grieving parents. A newspaper report of 28 April 1917 in the *Gazette* refers to the fact that '[Ernest] lost much blood *and but for the bravery of his orderly Private Black* [my emphasis], and of Sergeant Dow, who rendered first aid and conveyed him to a place of safety, he would have died'. This report, unlike one in the *Express* of the same date, is not evidently based on Colonel Innes's letter.

Secondly, Black was awarded the Distinguished Conduct Medal for the bravery which he displayed in dragging Ernest while under very severe fire to a place of safety and dressing his wounds. Such an award was not given on the basis of uncorroborated testimony – least of all the testimony of the man who was being recommended for the award.

Finally, the whole content of Black's statement ties in quite remarkably and without inconsistency with the detailed account in the Battalion history which was not published until many years later.

When Ernest had died, a telegram narrating the fact was sent from Le Touquet to the War Office in London and the army machine automatically sent a telegram on to Tom and Annie at Paisley. When Tom and Annie made their unhappy return to Paisley, they would arrive to find this wire waiting for them and repeating what they knew only too well:

DEEPLY REGRET TO INFORM YOU TE REID BLACK WATCH DIED APRIL EIGHTEENTH FROM SEPTICAEMIA FOLLOWING GUN SHOT WOUND RIGHT THIGH. THE ARMY COUNCIL EXPRESS THEIR SYMPATHY.

But help would be available for them. They were part of a large and close family which would rally round. They were devout Christians and, as Baptists, part of a particularly warm and supportive community. Tom would perforce have to throw himself into his work, Annie had a household to run and two other boys to look after, and both of them were involved in many organisations and activities which would require their presence. As brave a face would have to be put on as could be for the sake of the boys – and for the sake of all the friends and neighbours who had also lost loved ones or daily feared their loss.

One of the duties to which Tom had to return, and which would help to keep him going, was winding up Ernest's estate. He was very soon involved in correspondence with the War Office to establish what was due and to ingather it. To a layman, it might seem difficult to throw oneself into routine correspondence regarding the details of what was owed to one's son after so great a loss. But to a lawyer, a Scottish man of business, to do anything else would have seemed well nigh immoral as well as impractical. There were questions that required to be resolved. Payments due to Ernest had inadvertently been credited by Cox & Company, the army agents, to another officer with a similar name. There was also the question of the gratuity to which Ernest was entitled as a serving officer under Article 497 of the Royal Warrant for Pay. This had been calculated at the rate applicable to a Second Lieutenant, whereas Ernest had been promoted Acting Captain. On investigation by the War Office, it emerged that Ernest's promotion, which was not gazetted until 9 July 1917, after his death, was for one day only, 9 to 10 April 1917. Accordingly, when he died his rank was the substantive one of Second Lieutenant and the gratuity to which he was entitled was just £69.15s. His only financial reward for his one day's promotion was promotion pay of 10 shillings (50 pence).

Tom returned to correspondence with the War Office in January 1927, when he had come across a Field Message Book amongst Ernest's effects, which contained an entry showing that Ernest had made payments on behalf of 'A' Company from his own money amounting to 170 francs. Tom asked if the War Office would therefore 'remit me the equivalent of 170 francs which at 24 francs to the £ would amount to £7 1s 8d.' The War Office's reply was that as the company accounts and documents had been destroyed after being retained for the prescribed period, it was regretted that no adjustment could be made.

With that letter Ernest recedes from the pages of history into the realm of memory, less substantial but not forgotten, his presence emerging in the calm, confident gaze from his photographs, and reinforced by the annual tradition of the big waxy poppies.

In a letter to Tom, Colonel Innes wrote: 'Your son has died a hero's death for his country, doing his best and doing it extremely well and the country is much the poorer for his loss'. This clearly meant much to Tom, because he communicated the words *verbatim* to the *Express*.

From our standpoint, more cynical and more weary, we may reflect that commanding officers in the course of the bloodletting of the years on the Western Front must have used such a formula many times, and no doubt they did. But that does not mean that Ernest and perhaps thousands on both sides did not die heroes' deaths. He seems to me a quintessentially Scottish, reticent hero. He went into the War perfectly clear about its nature as he saw it: a struggle between good and evil. Despite all he knew at first hand of the slaughter and no doubt the mismanagement and the bungles, his courage and his optimism did not falter. His reaction to the horrors of France was to seek the even more dangerous life of an officer in the Royal Flying Corps. His spirits are reflected in the letters he wrote to Ronald, in the optimistic and cheerful letters to his parents from hospital before their arrival in France, in his pleasure that Jimmy Thomson, another good man, was coming out. His demeanour on the battlefield was strong and courageous, uncaring about his own safety, concerned for the progress of the advance, humane towards the defeated Germans. Cynicism never set in: he died an idealist for his ideals.

In 1923 a memoir was published of another young officer who had also been killed in France in 1917. He had written in May 1917 that 'Nothing but immeasurable improvements will ever justify all the damnable waste and unfairness of this war – I only hope those who are left will *never, never* forget at what sacrifice those improvements have been won'. The author of that memoir was the officer's cousin, Neville Chamberlain. Of course they did forget – after an armistice of only twenty years in the great civil war that racked Europe from 1914 to 1945. And they have forgotten since then and they forget again today. But it is too soon to say that the sacrifice was in vain. Many may find as I have done in the pity of war that is so real in the futility of the Western Front a more powerful argument against militarism than anything that has happened since. What is certain is that we shall not learn from that War, and the sacrifice will mean nothing, unless we remember it. Ernest has lain in the sandy soil of Étaples for 85 years now. He will not suffer any the more if we do not remember him, but our children and our grandchildren will. For their sake we should remember him. And for our sake we should remember him; for we are the poorer if we do not know those who went before us. And because Ernest turned aside so willingly from the future that would otherwise have been his and so readily accepted the rôle for which duty had shaped him, he is worthy of remembrance: for his own sake we should remember Ernest Reid.

Afterword to the Second Edition

I started writing this book ten years ago and it was first published in 2003. I greatly enjoyed writing it, and it has made me many friends and in some ways has altered the direction of my life. I'm glad that there is a demand for a second edition.

Apart from anything else, that has allowed me to make some reparation to Haig and the army he commanded in France from 1915 until the end of the war. In the first edition I was unfair to him and dismissive of the role he played in the 'learning curve', the change that took place in the army under his command. In part that was because I was anxious to highlight the role of the young officers at the front, rather than that of more exotic creatures on the staff. But the main reason was ignorance, pure ignorance.

When I subsequently spent some time studying Haig and his command and writing his biography,* I was sad to think how unfair I had been. In this edition the brief reference to Haig's achievement is more balanced. In all other respects the text is unaltered.

I also welcome the appearance of a second edition because it gives me an opportunity to say something more about Alexander Black, the soldier-servant who looked after Ernest so heroically. His military records do not survive, and in 2003 I concluded that it would have been good to have known more of him. A reader who is a professional genealogist responded unprompted and with great kindness, and as a result of Dennis White's researches I know much more about this brave and good man.

Alexander Black was born on 28 July 1879 in Forfar. His parents, who were not married, worked in a linen factory. He

---

* Walter Reid, *Architect of Victory: Douglas Haig*, Birlinn, Edinburgh, 2006, pbk 2009.

married Isabella Milne on 22 July 1904, and they had two children. Isabella died in 1912. His second wife was Elizabeth Ellis, whom he married on 2 June 1916. They had one son, born three years after the war. Alexander Black died in 1954.

Before the war he had started out working in a grocery, then repaired sewing machines and finally became an insurance superintendent, which remained his occupation after the war. He volunteered on 9 May 1916 and joined the Black Watch. He trained for two months in Dunfermline and a further three months in Nigg, and went off to France on 29 December 1916. After France he served in Palestine, and in addition to the DCM he had received in the field on the day after the Railway Triangle engagement, he was awarded the Military Medal in August 1919.

His great-grandson kindly gave me a photograph of Ernest's friend in Masonic regalia, solemn and direct. Alexander Black was staid and responsible, a strong family man when he returned home, and brave and reliable when he was at war.

Beauly
Bridge of Weir
24 January 2011

Further Reading

Lady Cynthia Asquith: *Diaries 1915–18*. Hutchinson, London, 1968

Arthur Banks: *A Military Atlas of the First World War*. Pen & Sword Books / Leo Cooper, London, 2001

Correlli Barnett: *The Swordbearers. Studies in Supreme Command in the First World War*. Eyre & Spottiswoode, London, 1963. Or Cassell, London, 2000

Bernard Bergonzi: *Heroes' Twilight. A Study of the Literature of the Great War*. Constable, London, 1965. Or Macmillan, London, 1980

The Black Watch Regiment – website: www/army.mod.uk/ blackwatch

C. Stewart Black: *The Story of Paisley*. J. & J. Cook, Paisley, 1952

Edmund Blunden: *Undertones of War*. Cobden-Sanderson, London, 1928. Or Collins, London, 1978

Brian Bond: *The Unquiet Western Front. Britain's Role in Literature And History*. Cambridge University Press, Cambridge, 2002

Brian Bond & Nigel Cave (eds): *Haig: A Reappraisal 70 Years On*. Pen & Sword Books/ Leo Cooper, London, 1999

Robert Brown: *The History of Paisley Grammar School from its foundation in 1576*. Alex Gardner, Paisley, 1875

Robert Brown: *The History of Paisley*. J. & J. Cook, Paisley, 1886

Yvonne Galloway Brown & Rona Ferguson (eds): *Twisted Sisters: Women, Crime & Deviance in Scotland since 1400*. Tuckwell Press, East Linton, 2002

Sylvia Clark: *Paisley: Threads of Time. A History*. Mainstream, Edinburgh, 1988

Colin Clifford: *The Asquiths*. John Murray, London, 2002

Rose E. B. Coombs: *Before Endeavours Fade: A Guide to the Battlefields of the First World War*. An After the Battle Publication, Battle Of Britain Prints International, London, 1994 (First edition 1976)

T. M. Devine: *The Scottish Nation: 1700–2000*. Allen Lane, London, 1999

Captain Cyril Falls (ed): *Military Operations France & Belgium 1917: The German Retreat to the Hindenburg Line and the Battle of Arras (History of the Great War Based on Official Documents)*, Vol. 1. Macmillan & Co., London, 1940

Niall Ferguson: *The Pity of War*. Allen Lane, London, 1998

Bernard Fergusson: *The Black Watch. A Short History*. The Black Watch Regiment, Perth, 1955. Revised edition 1985

Bernard Fergusson & John C. Stewart: *The Black Watch: A Brief Story of the Regiment from 1725 to the Present Day*. Heritage House Group Ltd, 1991

Colin Fox: *Monchy Le Preux*. Pen & Sword Books/ Leo Cooper, London, 2000

Sir Philip Gibbs: *The War Dispatches*. Anthony Gibbs & Phillips Ltd, London, 1966

Sir Martin Gilbert: *The First World War*. Weidenfeld & Nicolson, London, 1994

Douglas Gill & Julian Putkowski: *Le Camp Britannique d'Étaples*. Musée Quentovic, Étaples, n.d.

Robert Graves: *Goodbye to All That*. Jonathan Cape, London, 1929. Or Penguin Books, 1999

Paddy Griffith: *Battle Tactics of the Western Front: The British Army's Art of Attack, 1916–1918*. Yale University Press, Newhaven & London, 1994

Ian Hay: *The First Hundred Thousand*. William Blackwood & Sons, Edinburgh & London, 1915. Or Richard Drew, Glasgow, 1985

Holger H. Herwig: *The First World War. Germany and Austria–Hungary 1914–1918*. Arnold, London, 1997

Richard Holmes: *The Western Front*. BBC Books, London, 1999

Philip Howard: *Black Watch (Famous Regiment Series)*. Hamish Hamilton, London, 1968

John Jolliffe (ed): *Raymond Asquith: Life & Letters*. Collins, London, 1980

John Keegan: *The First World War*. Pimlico, London, 1999

Martin Kitchen: *The German Offensives of 1918*. Tempus Publishing, 2001

D. Lloyd George: *War Memoirs*. Ivor Nicholson & Watson, London, 1933–36. Or Simon Publications, London, 2001

Mary McCarthy: *A Social Geography of Paisley*. Paisley Public Library, Paisley, 1969

Catriona M. M. Macdonald and E. W. McFarland (eds): *Scotland and the Great War*. Tuckwell Press, East Linton, 1999

Frederick Manning: *The Middle Parts of Fortune. Somme and Ancre, 1916*. Piazza Press, London, 1929. Or Penguin, London, 2000

W. M. Metcalfe: *A History of Paisley*. Alex Gardner, Paisley, 1909

Robin Neillands: *The Great War Generals on the Western Front, 1914–18*. Robinson, London, 1999

Julian Putkowski: *Mutiny at Étaples*. www.shotatdawn.org.uk/etaples.htm

Walter Reid, Architect of Victory: Douglas Haig (Birlinn, Edinburgh, 2006; paperback 2009)

John Stuart Roberts: *Siegfried Sassoon*. Richard Cohen Books, London, 1999

Siegfried Sassoon: *Memoirs of a Fox-Hunting Man*. Faber & Gwyer, London, 1928

Siegfried Sassoon: *Memoirs of an Infantry Officer*. Faber & Faber, London, 1930

Siegfried Sassoon: *Sherston's Progress*. Faber & Faber, London, 1936

Siegfried Sassoon: *The Old Century and Seven More Years*. Faber & Faber, London, 1938

Siegfried Sassoon: *The Weald of Youth*. Faber & Faber, London, 1942

Siegfried Sassoon: *Siegfried's Journey*. Faber & Faber, London, 1945

Gary Sheffield: *Forgotten Victory. The First World War*. Myths & Realities. Headline, London, 2001

T. C. Smout: *A Century of the Scottish People, 1830–1950*. Collins, London, 1986

Sir Edward Spears: *Prelude to Victory*. Jonathan Cape, London, 1939

Tom Steel: *Scotland's Story*. Collins, London, 1984

Lt Colonel J. Stewart & John Buchan: *The Fifteenth (Scottish) Division, 1914–1919*. William Blackwood and Sons, Edinburgh & London, 1926

A. J. P. Taylor: *The First World War. An Illustrated History*. Hamish Hamilton, London, 1963

John Terraine: *Douglas Haig: The Educated Soldier*. Hutchinson, London, 1963. Or Cassell Military, London, 2000

Tim Travers: *The Killing Ground. The British Army, the Western Front and the emergence of modern warfare, 1900–1918*. Unwin Hyman, London, 1990

Barbara W. Tuchman: *August 1914*. Constable, London, 1962. Or Papermac, London, 1997

Peter Vansittart (selected by): *Voices from the Great War*. Jonathan Cape Ltd, London, 1981

Philip Warner: *World War One: A chronological narrative*. Arms & Armour Press, London, 1995

Major-General A. G. Wauchope (ed): *A History of the Black Watch [Royal Highlanders] in the Great War*. Medici Society, London, 1925–26

Denis Winter: *Haig's Command: A Reassessment*. Viking, London, 1991. Or Penguin Books, 2001

Denis Winter: *Death's Men. Soldiers of the Great War*. Allen Lane, London, 1978. Or Penguin Books, 1998

Leon Wolff: *In Flanders Fields*. Longmans Green & Co, London, 1959

Index